OSPREY

SPA124 *Lafayette 1*

American Volunteer Airmen in World War 1

OSPREY
PUBLISHING

SPA124 *Lafayette Escadrille*

American Volunteer Airmen in World War 1

Jon Guttman

Series editor Tony Holmes

Front Cover
On 19 September 1917 Sgts David McKelvie Peterson and Kenneth A Marr of SPA124, *l'Escadrille Lafayette*, spotted six Albatros scouts attacking a three-seater reconnaissance aeroplane of F44, flown by Sgts Desthuilleirs and Dauguet and Maréchal-des-Logis Viallet. They rushed to its assistance, and during the course of the fight an Albatros spiralled down out of control. Peterson, determined to see it crash, pursued the cripple to the ground, undaunted by the enemy ground fire that proceeded to pepper his SPAD at low altitude. The victory was credited to all five Allied participants, and Peterson was awarded the *Croix de Guerre* with palm for the extraordinary aggressiveness he displayed.

Typifying SPA124 practice at the time, the SPAD VII (S1331) that Marr flew on this day boasted a personal motif in the form of his initial, as well as the unit's definitive insignia of a Lakota (Sioux) Indian head. Peterson is said to have had a blue pennant aft of the Indian head, although photographs have yet to be found proving this, so his aircraft as depicted here is a reconstruction based on that description only.

Marr and Peterson both subsequently saw action with the US Army Air Service's 94th Aero Squadron, which the former led between 9 June and 25 September 1918. As commander of the 94th's A Flight, Peterson was credited with three more enemy aeroplanes destroyed. He then transferred to the 95th Aero Squadron on 16 May 1918, assuming command of the unit six days later. By war's end Peterson had raised his score to six kills (*Cover artwork by Mark Postlethwaite*)

First published in Great Britain in 2004 by Osprey Publishing
1st Floor Elms Court, Chapel Way, Botley, Oxford, OX2 9LP

ISBN 1 84176 752 2

Edited by Tony Holmes
Page design by Mark Holt
Cover Artwork by Mark Postlethwaite
Aircraft Profiles by Harry Dempsey
Origination by Grasmere Digital Imaging, Leeds, UK
Printed in Hong Kong through Bookbuilders

04 05 06 07 08   10 9 8 7 6 5 4 3 2 1

ACKNOWLEDGEMENTS
Thanks to Charles H Dolan and Col Marcel Robert, both former SPA124 members who have now 'Gone West'. Thank you also to those colleagues whose invaluable assistance in the scavenger hunt for photographs made this illustrated tome possible – Frank W Bailey, Jack Eder, Stephen T Lawson, Walter A Musciano, Greg Van Wyngarden and Radko Vasicek.

EDITORS NOTE
To make this series as authoritative as possible, the Editor would be interested in hearing from any individual who may have relevant photographs, documentation or first-hand experiences relating to the world's elite units, their pilots and their aircraft of the various theatres of war. Any material used will be credited to its original source. Please contact Tony Holmes via e-mail at: tony.holmes@osprey-jets.freeserve.co.uk

For details of all Osprey Publishing titles please contact us at:

Osprey Direct UK, PO Box 140, Wellingborough, Northants NN8 2FA, UK
E-mail: info@ospreydirect.co.uk

Osprey Direct USA c/o MBI Publishing, PO Box 1, 729 Prospect Ave, Osceola, WI 54020, USA
E-mail: info@ospreydirectusa.com

Or visit our website: www.ospreypublishing.com

CONTENTS

CHAPTER ONE
IDEALISTIC ORIGINS 6

CHAPTER TWO
INTO COMBAT 17

CHAPTER THREE
THE OBERNDORF RAID 47

CHAPTER FOUR
WITH *GROUPE DE COMBAT* 13 59

CHAPTER FIVE
SPLIT METAMORPHOSIS 96

CHAPTER SIX
VOLUNTEERS FOR JEANNE D'ARC 102

CHAPTER SEVEN
***LAFAYETTE* POSTSCRIPT 108**

APPENDICES 121
COLOUR PLATES COMMENTARY 124
BIBLIOGRAPHY 127

INDEX 128

IDEALISTIC ORIGINS

The date of 11 September was not a happy one for the United States in 2001, when two airliners, hijacked by Islamic terrorists, flew into the World Trade Center in New York City, and subsequently toppled both buildings to the ground. That same morning another hijacked airliner crashed into the Pentagon and a fourth crashed in western Pennsylvania after its passengers overpowered their captors.

That same date was little happier for a United States that was barely a year old, when Gen George Washington's Continental Army suffered a sound defeat at Brandywine Creek, Pennsylvania, on 11 September 1777, forcing the Americans to abandon their capital of Philadelphia to Maj Gen Sir William Howe's British Army.

Brandywine was not the outright rout that it might have been, however, for Washington's troops retreated in good order, thanks to inspired leadership by his lieutenants – including a young French volunteer.

Soon after the Declaration of Independence on 4 July 1776, French army Capt Marie Joseph Paul Yves Roch Gilbert du Motier, *marquis* de Lafayette, became so caught up in the ideals of liberty that he saw in the American colonists' revolt against Britain that he made arrangements through American plenipotentiary Silas Deane to travel there and offer his services to the Continental Congress without pay or rank.

At that time, the American delegation, led by Benjamin Franklin, was trying desperately to obtain French military aid and official recognition, but King Louis XVI was unwilling to commit himself to a war against Britain. Lafayette's offer, made without his country's sanction, was so appreciated by the Americans that he was commissioned a major general and subsequently proved his worth at Brandywine, rallying his faltering troops and even fighting alongside them, musket in hand, until wounded in the leg. After being led from the field, Lafayette – the Continental Army's youngest general, having turned 20 just five days before – went on to serve with distinction for the rest of the war. His example played a significant role in convincing France to recognise the United States on 8 February 1778.

The invaluable role that France played in the United States achieving independence in 1783 – and those French, such as Lafayette, who preceded their country to war – was very much on the minds of a number of Americans who offered their services to France soon after she entered the escalating European conflict that would become World War I. Some of them would form a fighter squadron, named for Lafayette, that would play a role similar to his in a reciprocal manner – by influencing the United States to enter the world conflict on France's side.

On 3 August 1914, brothers Kiffin and Paul Rockwell from Marion Country, South Carolina, contacted the French Consul-General in New Orleans, Louisiana, asking to join the French Army, departing for France four days later. On 5 August, William Thaw II signed an appeal for foreign volunteers. Elsewhere, Robert Soubiran steamed for France on 7 August to join the Foreign Legion. Soubiran's mother had died shortly

As with most of the *Escadrille Américaine's* first members, Kiffin Yates Rockwell had seen previous service in the trenches as a member of the French Foreign Legion (*SHAA B83.5686*)

Paul Ayres Rockwell, Kiffin's older brother, meets fellow Foreign Legionnaire Paul Pavelka in Paris in November 1915, shortly before the latter transferred into aviation, commencing flight training at Pau a month later. Prevented from joining the *Escadrille Américaine* by the severity of wounds he had suffered in December 1914, Paul Rockwell became the unit's official historian (*Greg Van Wyngarden*)

after his birth in Avallon, France on 16 March 1886, and in 1890 his father had brought him to New York City, where he became a US citizen on 10 August 1898. A proficient mechanic, Soubiran had worked for racing car driver Ralph de Palma until he felt compelled to fight for the land of his birth following the outbreak of war in Europe.

On 21 August 1914, the Foreign Legion accepted 42 Americans into its ranks, including Thaw, Jules James Bach, Weston Birch Hall, Robert Soubiran, Kiffin and Paul Rockwell and Gervais Raoul Lufbery.

New Yorker and Harvard University graduate Victor Chapman, who was studying architecture in Paris, was in Britain when war broke out, but he returned to France in September and joined the Legion. A devout Catholic who was uncertain of his purpose in life, Chapman was a knight in search of a crusade, and fighting for France provided him with one.

Fellow volunteer Edmond Charles Clinton Genet was the great-great grandson of Edmond Charles Genet, the French Republic's first minister to the United States in 1792. The latter had married the daughter of New York Governor DeWitt Clinton in 1794.

Born in Ossining, New York, on 9 November 1896, Edmond Genet joined the US Navy in December 1913, but after failing the examination to enter the US Naval Academy at Annapolis, he brooded over being the 'black sheep of the family' and wrote to his mother of his quest to

Sous-Lt William Thaw, a 'founding father' of the idea of an all-American volunteer squadron for the French air service prior to his own country's entry into World War 1, poses with a Nieuport 11 – probably his first with the new *escadrille* – at Luxeuil-les-Bains aerodrome in May 1916 (*SHAA B92.849*)

'be something worthwhile'. When World War 1 broke out, he began to express his conviction that the United States would soon enter the war, along with 'some hopes of dying for my country'.

On 14 December 1914, Genet was stirred by a sermon at St Paul's Cathedral in Boston relating to 'the present war and the relation of American Christians to it'. That, combined with his French heritage and the fact that his childhood sweetheart, Gertrude Talmage, was visiting Europe at the time, led Genet to desert from the Navy and, securing a passport from the French consul under the false pretence of being 21 (he was really only 18), he purchased passage aboard SS *Rochambeau* on 20 January 1915.

Although Genet enlisted in the Foreign Legion on 3 February, a friendship he struck up with fellow volunteer Norman Prince on the transatlantic voyage opened his eyes to aviation. For the time being, however, he fought in the Battle of Champagne on 22 September 1915 in the *3ème Regiment de Marche*, alongside fellow Soldat William Edward Dugan Jnr, the 25-year-old son of a shoe manufacturer from Patchogue, New York, who left a position with the United Fruit Company in Costa Rica when war broke out because he 'saw a chance to embark on a really great adventure'.

Bill Thaw, Norman Prince, Victor Chapman, Kiffin Rockwell and Edmond Genet epitomised an oft-cited element of the *Escadrille Lafayette's* myth – the image of pampered sons of wealthy, prominent American families who abandoned the material comforts of home for an idealistic cause. Such was certainly true of many of the volunteers, but others were drawn to the war out of a more primal sense of adventure, and the motives of two of the squadron's most peripatetic members, Weston 'Bert' Hall and Raoul Lufbery, remain something of an enigma.

Born on a farm near Higginsville, Missouri, on 7 November 1885, Bert Hall was the son of George Hall, who, at age 14, had served as an orderly for Confederate Col Jo Shelby during the Civil War, and had subsequently joined Shelby in Mexico fighting for another losing cause – that of Emperor Maximilian against Benito Juarez.

Largely driven by the exploits of his father, who he idolised, Bert Hall ran away from home to take on a number of occupations – a railroad hand, a chauffeur, a 'human cannon ball' at the Sell Brothers Circus and a merchant seaman, among others. As chance would have it, he was a taxi driver in Paris when war broke out, and promptly enlisted in the Foreign Legion. Often accused of being a liar, card cheat, con man and general scoundrel, Hall was to be the greatest exception to image of the young, almost naive *Lafayette* volunteer, although his combat record has always contradicted those less noble traits.

Raoul Lufbery was even more widely travelled and worldly wise than Hall, but the impression he made on his comrades included an air of mystery. 'I ate, slept, drank and fought beside him for months on end', said squadronmate Edwin C Parsons. 'I discussed combat tactics and played bridge and went on binges with him, but know him? Not a chance. In contrast to him, the Sphinx was a child's primer. He kept his real self shut up like a clam in a shell'.

Born in Clermont-Ferrand, France, on 21 March 1885, Gervais Raoul Victor Lufbery was the third son of New York chemist Edward Lufbery. Roaul's Parisian mother, Annette (Vesières) Lufbery, died before his first birthday, and after remarrying, his father moved back to the United States, leaving his three sons in the care of French relatives. After working in a chocolate factory, Raoul moved on to a number of jobs in North Africa, Turkey, the Balkans and Germany. In 1906, he and his brother Charles went to visit their father, then living in Wallingford, Connecticut, only to learn that Edward Lufbery, who also was a stamp dealer, had just departed for France! Raoul Lufbery would never meet his father.

After working for two years at a silver factory in Wallingford, Raoul set out for Cuba, then to New Orleans, where he worked as a baker. He went on to be a hotel waiter in San Francisco, served in the US Army in the

The pilots of N124 pose at full initial strength at Luxeuil in May 1916. They are, from left to right, Cpls Chapman and Cowdin, Sgt W Bert Hall, Sous-Lt Thaw, Capitaine Georges Thenault, Lt Alfred de Laage de Meux, Sgt Prince and Cpls Rockwell and McConnell. Sitting before Thenault and de Laage is Thenault's dog, Fram (*SHAA B96.135*)

Philippines, where he acquired his naturalised American citizenship, and won prizes as the best marksman in his regiment. Lufbery then moved on to jobs in Japan, China and India.

While in Calcutta in 1912, he met French exhibition flyer Marc Pourpe and became his mechanic, touring with him in China and Egypt, where Pourpe made a noteworthy round-trip flight from Cairo to Khartoum. Pourpe and Lufbery were in France to purchase a new Morane Saulnier parasol monoplane when war broke out, and Pourpe enlisted in the *Aéronautique Militaire*. As an American citizen, Lufbery enlisted in the Foreign Legion on 24 August, but one week later he transferred into the air service to rejoin Pourpe as his mechanic.

For fellow legionnaire Paul Pavelka, the war was only the latest in a life of adventures. Born to Russian immigrants in New York City on 26 October 1890, Pavelka had worked as a farmer, lumberman and handyman at a sanitarium, as well as a rancher in North Dakota and Montana. He had also tried to climb the Andes Mountains, shipped on a freighter to Japan, Australia and the South Pacific, and had been to Britain and the Continent. In 1912, Pavelka joined the US Navy and served aboard the battleship USS *Maryland*.

The outbreak of war found the recently discharged Pavelka in the Seaman's Home in New York. He first tried to join the British Army, and after being told that one had to be a British subject to do so, he joined a polyglot mob of 300 foreign volunteers bound for service with the Belgian Army until he arrived in France and decided to transfer to the more reliable Foreign Legion on 28 November 1914.

Assigned to the *1er Régiment* of the Moroccan Division near Reims, Pavelka soon met Kiffin Rockwell, and both survived the ill-fated assault on La Targette on 9 May 1915, although the latter was wounded in the right thigh. While convalescing in Paris, Rockwell met Thaw, who was then flying in C42, and who recommended that he also enter aviation. Rockwell took that advice and made the same suggestion to Pavelka, who had been bayoneted in the left leg on 16 June, before killing his German assailant. On 12 August both men took their preliminary physicals, and although Rockwell was sent for flight training at Avord on 4 September, Pavelka remained in the infantry until 27 November.

At least one American saw his first combat with the British rather than the French. James Norman Hall, born in Colfax, Iowa, on 22 April 1887, was in Beddgelert, Wales, when he learned that war had broken out. Passing himself off as a Canadian citizen, he enlisted in the 9th Battalion, Royal Fusiliers on 18 August 1914.

Shipped to France in May 1915, Hall fought in the trenches until 24 November, when he revealed his American nationality in order to be discharged and visit his father, who was suffering from Parkinson's disease. In Boston, Hall wrote a series of articles on his experiences for the *Atlantic* magazine, which would later be compiled into a book titled *Kitchener's Mob*.

By the end of 1914, several American *légionnaires*, like many other soldiers of the time, looked skyward for an alternative to the growing misery of trench warfare. On 10 December, James Bach entered the *Service Aeronautique*, obtaining his military flying licence, or *brevet militaire*, on 4 July 1915. Joining *escadrille* MS38 on 29 August, Cpl Bach had a disappointingly brief flying career, crashing while attempting to drop off two soldiers sent to spy on German forces behind enemy lines on 23 September. He thus became the first American airman to become a prisoner of war (PoW), although he would receive the *Légion d'Honneur*, *Médaille Militaire* and *Croix de Guerre* after the armistice.

Another *légionnaire*, Bill Thaw was the first to express ambitions that went beyond his own entry into the air service. Born the son of a wealthy business executive in Pittsburgh, Pennsylvania, on 12 August 1893, Thaw had left Yale University in 1911 to learn to fly. On 8 August 1913 he completed training at the Curtiss School of Aviation at Hammondsport, New York, and after purchasing a Curtiss Model E Hydro flying boat with his father's money, he pursued an aviation career in the United States and France.

After joining the Foreign Legion, Thaw's unit was shipped to the Chemin des Dames sector on 30 September 1914, where he served as a scout for his 17-man squad. That duty forced him to march three times as much as the others, for which Thaw soon found himself physically unsuited. He wished to enter aviation, and in October he told Paul Rockwell that he hoped to form a 'squadron of American volunteers'. On 24 December, Thaw transferred to Deperdussin-equipped *escadrille* D6, where he served as an observer, armed with a pistol and carbine. Later training at Saint-Cyr, he became the first American to obtain *brevet militaire* after qualifying in a Caudron G2 on 15 March 1915.

On 26 March Thaw returned to combat in C42, where he met Capitaine Georges Thenault. Born in Celle d'Evescault on 8 October 1888, Thenault had graduated from the officer academy at St Cyr in 1909, and served in the *Chasseurs Alpins* until 1913, when he took an interest in aviation. Obtaining his brevet on 26 December 1913, Thenault served as an observer in C11 and then as a pilot in C34, before taking command of C42 on 31 July 1915. On 21 February 1916, Thenault was credited with bringing down an enemy aeroplane over Bures, for which he was awarded the *Légion d'Honneur* and the medal of the Aero Club de France. During his time in C42, Thaw became good friends with Thenault, and came to admire his leadership qualities.

Bill Thaw's pre-war flying may have influenced a comrade-in-arms to enter aviation. Between battles, Bert Hall gained an early reputation as a colourful, but far-from-reliable, storyteller. In reaction of Thaw's tales of his flying exploits, Hall claimed to have learned to fly in 1909, and to have been the first to fly in the Turkish air service during the 1913 Balkan War. Later, after obtaining a transfer to the flight school at St Cyr, Hall had barely followed Thaw into the air when he crashed on the runway. When the French officer in charge of training extricated him from the wreckage and asked if he had ever been in an aeroplane before, Hall confessed that he had not.

'What in God's holy name do you mean', exclaimed the officer, 'starting off like that?'

'Well, I thought I might be able to fly', Hall replied. The French decided that anyone with that sort of nerve deserved another chance, and Hall finally did qualify in a Caudron on 19 August 1915. In early September he joined his *légionnaire* comrade James Bach at MS38, where they both were among the first 20 pilots to train in new Nieuport 10

Norman Prince's efforts, going on parallel to Thaw's, also influenced the French decision to form an American volunteer *escadrille,* and the decision of several of his acquaintances to join it (*Jon Guttman*)

two-seaters. On 1 January 1916, Hall departed to train on the even newer, single-seat Nieuport 11 *'Bébé'* fighter at Avord, becoming an instructor after completing the course.

A month after Thaw suggested the idea of an all-American *escadrille,* similar sentiments were expressed by another wealthy idealist. Born at Prides Crossing, Massachusetts, on 31 August 1887, Norman Prince was the son of an investment banker and industrialist. A graduate of Groton, Harvard College and the Harvard Law School, Prince took up law in Chicago, Illinois, in 1911, but his enthusiasm for it waned in favour of flying. His father scorned aviation as a distraction 'from the more serious concerns of life', but by training in secret, Prince earned Aero Club of America flying licence No 55 in 1912.

Often travelling to his family's estate at Pau, Prince came to regard France as his 'second country', and after war broke out he enrolled in the Burgess Flying School at Marblehead, Massachusetts, hoping to improve his skills before volunteering for French service. It was there that he mentioned his concept of an American volunteer squadron to friend, and colleague, Frazier Curtis in November 1914. On 18 January 1915 Prince departed for France aboard SS *Rochambeau,* along with Edmond Genet.

In Paris, Prince and a friend in the Paris Air Guard, Lt Jacques de Lesseps, tried to interest the French War Department in forming an American squadron. Among those he had sold on the idea were John J Chapman and Robert Chanler, father and uncle of Victor Chapman. On 4 March Prince joined the Foreign Legion, then transferred into aviation, receiving his *brevet militaire* on a Voisin at Pau on 1 May and immediately being assigned to VB108 at Nancy.

Promoted to sergeant in June, Prince transferred to VC113, whose Voisins were armed with 37 mm cannons, on 1 July. His friend Frazier Curtis was less fortunate, suffering two crashes at Avord and being invalided out with a nervous breakdown. While in Paris, however, Curtis persuaded the director of the American Ambulance Corps, physician Dr Edmund Louis Gros, to support his and Prince's American squadron concept. Although Curtis would ultimately be granted a honourable discharge from the French Army on 8 August 1915, his efforts, combined with those of Dr Gros and others, advanced the idea through the French military.

On 3 May 1915, Prince was joined at VB108 by Elliot Christopher Cowdin, the 29-year-old son of a ribbon manufacturer from Far Rockaway, New York. A Harvard graduate, Cowdin had enlisted in the American Ambulance Service in December 1914 and served alongside the 1st Cavalry Division of the Belgian Army until February 1915, when, after meeting Prince in Paris, he joined the French air service through the Foreign Legion. Cowdin's high spirits often manifested themselves in poor discipline and a tendency to pick brawls with his comrades, but in the air he applied his aggressive nature to the enemy. On 9 July he was awarded the *Croix de Guerre* with star for attacking two German aircraft on 26 June, damaging one and emerging with his own aeroplane damaged and his flying helmet holed by enemy bullets.

On 8 August, Cowdin was joined at VB108 by Victor Chapman, who after 11 months in the trenches had found himself transferred – largely through his father's and uncle's influence – into aviation. Initially serving as a bombardier-gunner, Chapman entered flight training at Avord on 26 September. There, he found a kindred spirit in Kiffin Rockwell, and he also met Bert Hall, who was then serving as a flying instructor.

While Chapman was earning his *brevet* (on 9 January 1916) in a Maurice Farman, his uncles, William Astor and Robert Chanler, were helping Prince with his programme to start an American unit – and using their considerable financial and political influence to ensure that Chapman would be one of its first members.

Rockwell had by then earned his *brevet* (on 22 October 1915), after which he quickly converted onto the Nieuport alongside Chapman, graduating at the head of his class. He had learned of the deaths of many *légionnaire* comrades while undergoing his training, and in November 1915 he wrote in a letter to a friend that 'I have many scores to settle, and there is going to be more than one "Boche" aviator to settle them, or I will not live to tell the tale'.

Cpl Elliott C Cowdin stands beside a Nieuport 11 decorated with oblique blue, white and red bands on its fuselage while serving with N65. Cowdin claimed his only victory while flying with this unit on 20 April 1916 (*SHAA B76.1358*)

On 15 August 1915 Cowdin took up pursuit training, after which he was assigned firstly to N38 and then, on 12 November, N49. During a month's leave, Cowdin, Prince and Thaw went to New York on 23 December, where they were mobbed by newspaper reporters, each with their own agenda – either lionising their example as a call for the United States to join the Allied cause, or condemning their participation as a violation of American neutrality. Norman Prince persuaded his 30-year-old elder brother Frederick Henry Prince Jnr to enlist in the Foreign Legion on 16 January 1916. By the time the volunteers returned to the front, the French government fully appreciated their propaganda value and took more serious steps toward forming an all-American unit.

After rejoining N49, Cowdin transferred to N65 in February 1916, and Thaw joined him there on 26 March. During the fighting over Verdun, Cowdin was cited for attacking 12 German aircraft and shooting down an LVG on 4 April, for which he became the first American to be awarded the *Médaille Militaire*, as well as a second palm for his *Croix de Guerre*.

Raoul Lufbery's interest in learning to fly was one of the few things about which he made no secret. On 2 December 1914, Marc Pourpe fatally crashed while trying to land at night in fog. In spite of its accidental nature, Lufbery blamed the Germans for his friend's death, and promptly enrolled in the aviation training school at Chartres, where he earned his *brevet militaire* in a Maurice Farman on 29 July 1915.

After further training at Amberieu, he joined VB106, flying Voisin bombers, but later requested training in Nieuports. His flying was initially so ham-fisted that he was almost returned to reconnaissance duties, but he persisted and ultimately qualified as a fighter pilot. It was to be the final, defining decision of his life. 'I only know one certain thing about him', Edwin Parsons later wrote. 'Raoul Lufbery lived, fought and died for revenge'.

The most experienced candidate for the American *escadrille* was Didier Masson, who had been born in Asniéres, France, on 23 February 1886, and who had served in the *129e Régiment d'Infanterie* between 1904 and 1906. In 1909, he became mechanic for aviator Louis Paulhan, and performed his first solo flight in a Farman later that year.

Masson moved to Los Angeles, California, in 1910, and in addition to exhibition and test flying, he flew a Glenn Martin pusher for Maj Gen Alvaro Obregón during the Mexican Revolution – and made one of history's first air attacks on a warship when he tried to bomb the Federal gunboat *General Guerrero* on 10 May 1913. Masson quit his first stint as a mercenary pilot on 5 August, claiming that he had not been paid in a month, and that he did not want to obey an order from Obregón to bomb cities.

On 8 September 1914, Masson returned to France, re-enlisted in the *129ème Régiment*, served briefly in the *36ème*, then began flight training at Pau in October, obtaining his *brevet* in a Caudron on 10 May 1915. After serving in C18, he left in September 1915 to train in Nieuports, joined N68 in April 1916, but was assigned to Cazeaux as an instructor on 16 April.

Ironically, while Masson was flying for Obregón in Mexico, a future squadronmate was offering his services to Obregón's rival. Born in Holyoke, Massachusetts, on 24 September 1892, Edwin Charles Parsons was the son of an insurance broker and a direct descendent of Coronet Parsons, a founder of Springfield, Massachusetts, in 1636. Parsons attended the University of Pennsylvania, intending to work in his father's business, but became bored and moved to southern California, where he worked as a rancher and a gold miner. In 1912 Parsons met Glenn Curtiss and was inspired to make his first flight on 12 July that same year. He had mastered the aeroplane by late 1913, when he was contacted by Villista agents, who offered him payment in gold to teach some of Pancho Villa's men to fly.

After 11 frustrating months as an instructor, combined with some reconnaissance flights, Parsons was en route to obtain spare parts for a wrecked aeroplane when a German agent, running a cigar shop in Chihuahua, informed him that Villa was planning to attack Americans across the border. Parsons took the hint and terminated his association with Villa.

He tried to resume studies at the University of Philadelphia, but in the spring of 1915 he learned from a female news reporter that steps were underway to form an all-American volunteer squadron in France. His father objected, stating that it was 'not our war', but Parsons managed to get aboard the liner *Carpathia* with a shipment of 2000 horses by posing as an assistant veterinarian. After serving for a time in the American Ambulance Service, he was accepted into the air service through the Foreign Legion on 13 April 1916, obtaining his *brevet* on 23 August.

Two other Americans entered French squadrons prior to the formation of an all-American *escadrille*, while other future squadronmates were also arriving in France. Although Horace Clyde Balsley had been born in

Carbondale, Pennsylvania, on 27 July 1893, his father, Episcopal rector Enos Josiah Balsley, moved to San Antonio, Texas, in 1907. Clyde graduated with honours from the West Texas Military Academy, but left the University of Texas at Austin when his father became invalided with arteriosclerosis, from which he died in 1914. Although his father had hoped he would follow him into the ministry, Clyde wanted to become involved in the European war and aviation, which he called 'the newest game in the world', and he departed in January 1915.

Making his way into the American Ambulance Service on 1 May, Balsley served as a driver and mechanic until 28 September, when he and fellow ambulance volunteer Dudley Lawrence Hill (the 23-year-old son of the founder of the Union Stove Works at Peekskill, New York), arrived at Pau for flight training. They were joined the next day by Charles Chouteau Johnson, a 27-year-old descendant of the founder of his home city of St Louis, Missouri.

While studying law at the University of Virginia in Charlottesville, 'Chute' Johnson had met James Rogers McConnell from Chicago, Illinois. The latter was both a brilliant student and a prankster who was appointed 'King of the Hot Foot Society' and voted president of the university's Aero Club. McConnell graduated with a law degree in 1910, as did Johnson in 1913, and the two tried to go into business together in New York.

After working as a land and industrial agent for the Randolph and Cumberland Railroad in Carthage, North Carolina, as well as serving as a lieutenant in the state militia, McConnell decided to go to France in January 1915. Here, he became a driver in the American Ambulance Service, and on 5 October he was awarded the *Croix de Guerre* with star for 'courage and fearlessness worthy of the highest praise'.

Johnson, too, went to France, probably inspired by the example of his mother's brother Pierre Chouteau, who had served in the Foreign Legion during the Franco-Prussian War of 1870-71. Joining the American Ambulance Service in early 1915, Johnson transferred to the Foreign Legion that summer and entered the air service on 2 September.

Training at Pau, Balsley and Johnson got their *brevets* on 2 January 1916, and after training in Voisins at Amberieu, both were assigned to V97 on the 26th. While defending Paris from Zeppelin attacks, Balsley and Johnson learned of the plans to form an American *escadrille*, and applied to be part of it.

Jimmy McConnell also wished to take on a more active role. Joining the Foreign Legion on 1 October 1915, he transferred into aviation, trained at Pau and earned his *brevet* on 6 February 1916. On 16 April he completed training in Nieuports and, having made the acquaintance of Victor Chapman and Kiffin Rockwell, he managed to get an immediate assignment to the newly-forming *escadrille Americaine*.

Another candidate for the new unit was Lawrence Dana Rumsey Jnr, the 29-year-old son of a tannery, railroad and banking tycoon from Buffalo, New York. Graduating from Harvard in 1908, Rumsey was a professional polo player before the war, but in late 1914 he joined the American Ambulance Service and saw action in both France and Belgium between January and July 1915. He switched to the air service via the Foreign Legion on 9 September, and began training at Pau two days later.

Some of the first members of N124 line up before the *escadrille's* first aircraft – a Nieuport 10 – newly delivered for training purposes in April 1916. They are, from left to right, Cpls James R McConnell and Kiffin Rockwell, Capitaine Georges Thenault, Sgt Norman Prince and Cpl Victor Chapman (*SHAA B89.2224*)

After a good start, Rumsey crashed twice during his *tour de piste* (a test of navigation over a triangular course), which delayed him receiving his *brevet* until 2 February 1916.

Finally, on 14 March 1916, the dream of Thaw and Prince became reality as Col Henri Regnier, director of French military aeronautics, announced plans to organise an *escadrille Americaine*, with Clyde Balsley, Victor Chapman, Elliot Cowdin, Charles C Johnson, James McConnell, Norman Prince, Kiffin Rockwell, Lawrence Rumsey and William Thaw as its first pilots. On 16 April *Escadrille* N124 was officially formed, with an altered membership roster – Balsley, Johnson and Rumsey had been placed on a replacement list, and their places in the unit taken by Bert Hall and two Frenchmen, who were to serve as the squadron's commander and second-in-command.

Thaw had asked his old commander from C42, Capitaine Thenault, to apply for the new unit, and he was so appointed on 9 April. The squadron's executive officer, Lt Alfred de Laage de Meux, was the scion of generations of French warriors, and had previously served in the *14ème Regiment de Dragons*, with which he was wounded in the thigh on 31 August 1914 and rescued by his orderly, Cpl Jean Dressy.

After his recovery, de Laage joined C30 as an observer in March 1915, downing a German aeroplane in June 1915 and earning a second palm to his *Croix de Guerre*. Training in his spare time to fly a Farman, de Laage obtained a unique pilot's *brevet* without formal instruction on 22 October. He then trained on Nieuports and re-entered combat over Verdun. Based on his record, and because de Laage spoke fluent English, Thenault asked him to join the new unit, and de Laage's faithful orderly, Dressy, also came on as a mechanic.

INTO COMBAT

On 20 April 1916, N124's personnel arrived in Luxeuil les Bains, in the *VIIème Armée* sector. Also serving as home base to Capt Maurice Happe's group of Farman and Voisin bombers, Luxeuil was one of the best aerodromes in France, occupying two miles of flat field surrounded by foothills of the Vosges Mountains, near the Swiss border. Its pilots stayed in a beautiful villa adjoining Luxeuil's hot baths.

N124's first aeroplane was a war-weary Nieuport 10 bequeathed it by N49, based at nearby Fontaine, for training purposes. It did not last long, for Prince – who suffered from faulty eyesight – crashed it into a hangar, emerging miraculously unhurt. In the first week of May, the *escadrille* received three new Nieuport 16s, powered by 110-hp Le Rhône rotary engines, which Thenault allotted to de Laage, Thaw and himself. An identical number of Nieuport 11s, fitted with 80-hp Le Rhônes, also arrived at the same time. The fighters had a maximum speed in the vicinity of 100 mph, and two hours' endurance. Armament consisted of a single Lewis machine gun mounted above the wing to fire over the propeller arc.

In one of his letters, Chapman described the new fighters as mostly being camouflaged in mottled light and dark brown, as well as light and dark green, but that his 80-hp machine was a solid cream colour. Hall wrote that the undersurfaces of his Nieuport were painted sky blue.

Capt Thenault believed in easing his new pilots into combat gradually, and later criticised squadron commanders of the US Army Air Service (USAS) for doing too much too soon, resulting in heavy initial casualties. Later, as his first cadre of pilots became more experienced, he gave them more leadership responsibilities while he attended to the administrative burdens of running the squadron. The latter would soon include presiding over the funerals of members killed in action or accidents, and selecting replacements from a growing pool of eager volunteers.

Thenault's position, which required him to judge the right balance of discipline and latitude for his high-spirited men, compelled him to set an emotional barrier between himself and them, with the exception of Sous-Lt Thaw. Thenault, in turn, commanded the respect of his men, save whenever he tried to play the piano – an invariably futile effort that would draw howls of protest even from his faithful dog, Fram.

As the Nieuports began to arrive, Kiffin Rockwell took Bert Hall's assigned, but still unarmed, aeroplane for a two-hour flight to the lines on 29 April. Rockwell and Chapman flew two reckless – and fruitless – searches for the enemy on 5 and 9 May, and it was not until 13 May that N124 flew its first *official* patrol over the lines, with Cpl Rockwell leading Thenault, Thaw, Chapman and McConnell from a point three miles from the Swiss border to Mulhouse at an altitude of 10,000 ft. Aside from being fired upon by anti-aircraft batteries southwest of Mulhouse, the sortie was uneventful, but for Chapman, it was an epiphany – the knight-errant had indeed found his crusade, and the weapon with which to pursue it.

The next day saw a visit by a French Army motion picture unit, as well as a newspaper reporter whose grotesquely exaggerated article disgusted

N124 members prepare for a patrol before the French newsreel cameras at Luxeuil in May 1916. They are, from left to right, Chapman, Cowdin, Weston Bert Hall, Thaw, unidentified, Prince, unidentified mechanic, unidentified, Rockwell and an unidentified squadron member (*Greg VanWyngarden*)

the Americans when they read it. It would not be the last distorted, or outright false, account through which they would have to wince in the months and years to come.

The considerable film footage taken that day reveals that most of the pilots had already adopted personal markings for their aircraft – a practice that would remain in effect even after N124 adopted a squadron insignia, in contrast to the more usual French policy of using numerals for individual identification. Among others, Cowdin (flying Nieuport 16 serial No N1154), Hall (with N1205), Prince (N574) and Rockwell applied their initials in white to the fuselage sides and/or upper decking, while McConnell used *MAC* on his aeroplane. One Nieuport (possibly Thaw's) had white discs on the fuselage sides and wheel hubs, but Chapman never chose a personal motif.

During his fourth patrol, on 18 May, Rockwell experienced engine trouble and was just turning for home when he spotted an LVG two-seater 2000 ft below him. As he dived directly on his quarry, the German pilot turned for his lines while his gunner fired at Rockwell's Nieuport, striking a wing spar. Ignoring the damage, the American closed to point-blank range and fired just four Lewis rounds, before turning away barely in time to avoid a collision. Incredibly, the two-seater went into a vertical dive and crashed in flames near Thann.

A French observation post telephoned Luxeuil to confirm N124's first aerial victory, and by the time Rockwell landed, his cheering comrades were waiting to carry him around in triumph. His brother Paul, who was in Paris when he heard the news, rushed to Luxeuil with an 80-year-old bottle of bourbon whiskey. After drinking a shot, Rockwell offered one to Chapman, but he declined, suggesting instead that each pilot be 'entitled to one slug' of the 'Bottle of Death' every time he shot down an enemy aeroplane.

Having proved its mettle in a relatively quiet sector, N124 was ordered to leave Luxeuil on 19 May to support Gen Robert Nivelle's *IIème Armée* near Verdun. The squadron's new aerodrome at Behonne was situated on a plateau, surrounded by deep ravines. The pilots stayed in a stone villa between the airfield and the town of Bar-le-Duc.

On 22 May Thaw was promoted to full lieutenant. That same day, Nivelle launched a counteroffensive to retake Fort Douaumont, and N124 was temporarily attached to *Groupe de Combat* (GC) 12 to provide the morning air cover. Adjutant Bert Hall was flying his second sortie of the day when he became separated from his flight. He then encountered an Aviatik two-seater at 12,000 ft above Malancourt and forced it down to 3000 ft while its observer sent tracers through his wings and within a foot of his cockpit. Diving under the enemy's tail, Hall fired two bursts into the Aviatik's underside and saw it fall in pieces near the French frontline trenches. Almost a month later, he received the *Médaille Militaire* and the *Croix de Guerre* with palm for scoring N124's second confirmed victory.

While leading the first morning patrol on 24 May, Thaw surprised a Fokker E III and brought it down north of Vaux. Later that same morning, Thenault was leading Chapman, de Laage, Thaw and Rockwell on a second sortie when they encountered 12 German aircraft over Etain. Chapman, too eager to await Thenault's signal, promptly dived at the enemy, followed by Rockwell and Thaw.

Chapman claimed a Fokker out of control before being wounded in the arm, while Rockwell's windscreen was hit and his face was lacerated by glass and bullet fragments. Wiping the blood from his goggles, he claimed an enemy aeroplane before returning to Behonne, his fuel almost exhausted. Thaw also claimed a Fokker before his Lewis gun jammed. As he turned back, he came under fire from two pursuing Aviatiks, which put a bullet through his left elbow and his fuel tank. Petrol spurted over his

Kiffin Rockwell tests the overhead Lewis machine gun on his Nieuport 11 at Luxeuil in late April 1916. He scored N124's first victory on 18 May 1916 (*SHAA B75.613*)

This line-up photograph of N124 Nieuports at Behonne in June 1916 shows the personal motifs that remained a unit trademark even after the *escadrille* became a US Army Air Service squadron in 1918. Nieuport 11 N1116 'P' was Prince's aeroplane, Nieuport 16 N1154 'C' was Cowdin's, Nieuport 11 N1247 bore the Texas 'Lone Star' of Cpl H Clyde Balsley and Nieuport 11 N1286 *RUM* was flown by Sgt Lawrence Rumsey (*George H Williams Collection via Greg VanWyngarden*)

legs and feet, and as he reached forward to cut off the engine, he realised that his arm was broken. Gliding over the lines, Thaw pancaked near Fort Travennes, was taken to the hospital at Neuilly and subsequently convalesced at his sister's residence in Paris.

Valuing their fearlessness over their rash insubordination, the French promoted Chapman and Rockwell to sergeant for their actions on 24 May. In addition, Chapman received the *Croix de Guerre*, Rockwell the *Médaille Militaire* and *Croix de Guerre* with palm and Thaw was made a *Chevalier de la Légion d'Honneur*. Chapman was back in action in 24 hours, but Thenault sent Rockwell to hospital for 15 days, eight of which he spent in Paris recovering at the apartment of Mrs Alice Weeks.

With Thaw out of commission for a longer period, Thenault called for a replacement from the reserve pool, and later that day Raoul Lufbery

Sgt Lawrence Dana Rumsey Jnr poses before his Nieuport 11 N1286 in July 1916. Note the light-coloured elevators and left lower wing – probably replacements for the damaged originals (*H H Wynne*)

McConnell and his *mécanicien* pose beside his Nieuport 11, on which he had recently replaced his original *MAC* marking with the footprint which represented the University of Virginia's 'Hot Foot Society' (*Jack Eder Collection*)

arrived. The *escadrille's* ranks were expanded further by the arrival of Clyde Balsley and Charles C Johnson on the 29th, with Lawrence Rumsey joining on 4 June and Dudley Hill five days later.

After Balsley received Nieuport 11 No 1247 on 8 June, he painted a white 'Lone Star of Texas' on its fuselage and wheel hubs, while Johnson similarly applied dice with a single black spot to 1434. Rumsey's Nieuport 11s, No 1286 and later 1290, bore a white chevron band across the upper wing and the name *RUM* on the fuselage. By then McConnell had replaced *MAC* with a white footprint on his Nieuport, referring to his collegiate 'Hot Foot Society'.

While on a patrol on 17 June, Chapman spotted a formation of German aircraft on the opposite side of the Meuse River, and again ignoring Thenault's orders for prudence, he dived to the attack, compelling his comrades to follow. In the ensuing melée, Chapman became separated from the others, and after landing at Vadelaincourt to refuel, he took off alone to look for trouble. He found it in the form of two enemy two-seaters, one of which he forced to land near Béthincourt, although it was not confirmed.

At that point, three Fokkers that had been escorting the two-seaters shook off their surprise at the lone Nieuport's attack and pounced. Chapman was replacing his Lewis magazine when a bullet severed his right

Curiously, Rumsey's Nieuport N1290 looks identical to N1286. The rudder might also have been damaged and replaced (*National Archives*)

aileron control rod and creased his skull. He fell into a spin, convincing his antagonists that he was finished, but once out of range Chapman grabbed the ends of the control rods and, controlling the stick with his knees, landed safely at Froidos aerodrome.

In a letter to his brother Paul, Kiffin Rockwell – who had resumed patrolling on 10 June – mentioned the possibility that German ace Oswald Boelcke had hit Chapman. Boelcke and his unit, *Flieger Abteilung* (F. Fl. Abt.) 62, were operating from Sivry at the time, but he was not credited with anything on 17 June. Another 'rising star' did, however – Ltn Walter Höhndorf of *Kampfeinsitzer Kommando* (KEK) Vaux, claimed a Nieuport in French lines for his fifth of an eventual fourteen victories.

After having his wound dressed and his aeroplane repaired, Chapman returned to Behonne at 1530 hrs and asked to join the 1600 hrs patrol. Thenault refused, instead urging him to go for further treatment at the hospital. Chapman, concerned that he would be dropped from the squadron roster, ignored his CO's advice, and the offer of a short rest leave in Paris. Thenault then resorted to bribery, assigning him new 110-hp Nieuport 16 No 1334. That kept Chapman both happy and temporarily out of the air, while he personally saw to the new machine's readiness and also had his mechanic remove its earth camouflage and repaint it in an overall pale grey finish.

On 18 June Thenault was leading Prince, Rockwell and Balsley on a dawn sortie to protect *reglage* (artillery spotting) aircraft when the quartet encountered a large German formation north of Verdun. Balsley closed to within 50 metres of an Aviatik, only to suffer a gun jam after firing just one round. As he turned away to clear it, he found himself in a crossfire from four enemy aeroplanes. Balsley tried to loop into a cloud, but a bullet struck him in the right thigh and fragmented, sending splinters into his intestines, kidneys and lungs. His Nieuport fell into an inverted spin at 12,000 ft, but using his hands to work his stricken leg, he was able to level

Balsley, Prince, McConnell and recently arrived Cpl Gervais Raoul Lufbery chat next to Cowdin's Nieuport 16 at Behonne in June 1916. The rudder of Prince's Nieuport 11 N1116 'P' can be seen in the foreground (*George H Williams Collection via Greg VanWyngarden*)

out and dived for Allied territory. Upon landing between the lines, Balsley's undercarriage caught on some barbed wire and the plane flipped over. As German artillery began targeting his Nieuport, Balsley grasped at bits of grass to crawl away until a French soldier came out and dragged him to his trench.

Balsley was taken to hospital at Vadelaincourt, where the French surgeon presented him with six bullet fragments that he had removed. He required more operations, however, and he suffered from thirst as well as

Balsley, Lufbery, Cpl Dudley L Hill, Prince, Cowdin and McConnell strike a sober pose at Béhonne. The mood would be even more sombre after 18 June, when Balsley was grievously wounded, bringing the realities of aerial warfare home to the squadron for the first – but by no means last – time (*SHAA B93.4228*).

Norman Prince poses beside Cowdin's Nieuport 16 N1154. Note the rack for extra Lewis gun ammunition drums alongside the cockpit (*Charles Woolley via Greg VanWyngarden*)

pain because of his perforated intestine. When Vic Chapman brought Balsley's toothbrush to the hospital on the 21st and learned of his being unable to drink water, he asked, 'How about oranges?' The doctor assented, and although none were available in the village, Chapman promised to bring Balsley the oranges if he had to go to Paris to find them.

Chapman made a rough landing when he returned from the morning patrol on 23 June, breaking a strut. While his mechanic repaired it, Chapman left the field, but returned at 1215 hrs carrying a bundle of newspapers containing chocolate and two bags of oranges. His Nieuport 16 was repaired, and as he took off to join Thenault, Lufbery and Prince on the next mission, he informed his mechanic that he planned to take the parcels to Balsley at Vadelaincourt upon his return. 'See you soon', he said. 'I shall not be long'.

That evening Balsley got his oranges, but it was Cowdin who brought them, stating that Chapman's aeroplane had broken down. Only later did Balsley learn the truth.

The afternoon patrol ran into five German aircraft northeast of Douaumont, and after a brief fight, the N124 pilots returned to Behonne.

One of Germany's early Fokker aces, Ltn Kurt Wintgens of *Flieger Abteilung* 6 inflicted the first fatality upon N124 when he shot down Sgt Victor Chapman on 23 June 1916 for his seventh victory. Wintgens received the *Orden Pour le Mérite* and had raised his score to 19 by the time he was shot down and killed by Lt Alfred Heurteaux of N3 on 25 September 1916 (*SHAA B82.505*)

Unknown to the others, however, Chapman had not disengaged, and a Maurice Farman crew reported seeing a lone Nieuport attacking an enemy fighter when three more jumped it. The Nieuport pilot fought on until one of his antagonists drove him down out of control to crash at Haumont near Samoneux, six kilometres inside German lines. The first American airman to die in French service was probably the seventh of an eventual 19 victories credited to Ltn Kurt Wintgens of F. Fl. Abt. 6. Chapman's body was never positively identified, and his crypt in the *Lafayette Escadrille* memorial remains empty.

The loss of Vic Chapman was a blow to everyone in N124, and most of all to Rockwell. 'Last night I went to bed', he wrote a friend, 'but I couldn't sleep, thinking about him, especially as his bed was right beside mine'. The next day, he wrote, 'I am afraid it is going to rain tomorrow, but if not, Prince and I are going to fly about ten hours and do our best to kill one or two Germans for Victor'.

On 19 June N124 got a replacement for Balsley in the person of Didier Masson. On the 25th Cowdin departed, officially due to 'ill health', since Thenault was unwilling to put in writing anything that would shed

Joining N124 on 19 June 1916 as a replacement for Balsley, Sgt Pierre Didier Masson had already flown as a mercenary in the service of Mexican Brig Gen Alvaro Obregón in 1913, prior to serving in French *escadrilles* C18 and N68 (*Lafayette Foundation*)

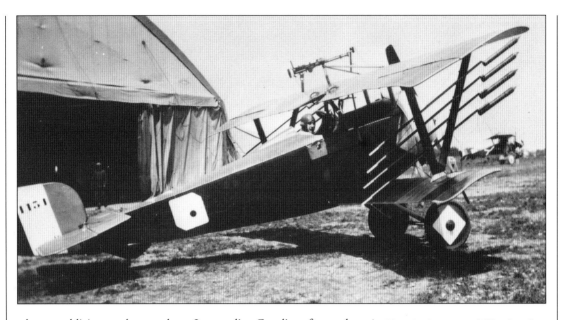

adverse publicity on the squadron. In actuality Cowdin, after such a promising start in N65, had become a troublemaker, more prone to fighting with his comrades on the ground than Germans in the air, and with a tendency to go off on long, unauthorised leaves. Cowdin continued to drift from one assignment to another in the French and US Army air services until his official discharge from the latter on 28 December 1918, and did little thereafter besides pursue polo until his death from bronchial pneumonia on 6 January 1933.

Although its members flew continuously to avenge Chapman and Balsley, official success seemed to elude N124 over the next month. On 30 June, for example, McConnell and Lufbery claimed an enemy aeroplane out of control over Verdun. On another, McConnell saw 'Nimmie' Prince burn a balloon using wing-mounted Le Prieur rockets, but it occurred six miles behind enemy lines and there were no other Allied witnesses.

After the departure of Elliot Cowdin for reasons of 'ill health', his Nieuport 16 (N1434) went to Sgt Charles Chouteau Johnson. Photographed at Cachy aerodrome, it sports a 'snake eyes' dice emblem and Le Prieur rockets for balloon-busting missions (*SHAA B77.1390*)

On enforced convalescent leave from N65, Sous-Lt Charles Nungesser (centre, smoking a cigarette) attached himself to N124 on 14 July 1916 in order to keep flying. Norman Prince is at left and Didier Masson at right (*SHAA B82.2326*)

This photograph, taken at Behonne in July 1916, shows, from left to right, de Laage, Charles Chouteau Johnson, Rumsey, McConnell, Thaw, Lufbery, Rockwell, Didier Masson, Prince and Hall. The slight distance between Bert Hall and the others suggests that he may already have been ostracised for his crude language and suspected cheating at cards (*Greg VanWyngarden*)

Nungesser poses beside Nieuport 17 N1490, which he flew while attached to N124. On 21 July 1916 he downed an Aviatik for his 11th victory (*SHAA B89.3596*)

When the *escadrille* finally did log its next confirmed victory, it came from a visitor from Cowdin's old outfit. On 22 June 1916, the already legendary Sous-Lt Charles Nungesser of N65 had downed two Aviatiks over Lamorville, but ended up crash-landing near his victims. That led to his third visit to the hospital since the outbreak of war, with a broken nose and jaw, a dislocated knee and bullet fragments in his lip. N65 had him on an enforced sick leave, but Nungesser was soon bored with convalescence and so, on 14 July, he celebrated Bastille Day by flying to Behonne and asking to be placed on N124's roster.

That evening he appeared in the *l'Escadrille Americaine* mess looking resplendent in an impeccably tailored, bemedalled black uniform, outshone only by the double row of gold teeth gleaming from between his scarred lips. Although his American friends were suitably impressed when he tore a deck of cards in half, Nungesser needed a heavy cane to limp to his Nieuport 17.

Kiffin Rockwell climbs aboard Hall's Nieuport 11 N1205, which displays the latter's initial on the fuselage upper decking and an unusual camouflage pattern on the upper wing (*Jon Guttman*)

During a patrol on 21 July, Nungesser engaged an Aviatik, and its Fokker escort, shooting the two-seater down near Seuzey and sending the fighter fleeing for home.

On the same day Rockwell dived on a German aeroplane, only to be attacked by another, which was dived upon in turn by Hall. 'It was a parade downward, everyone shooting at once', McConnell wrote in a letter to Alice Weeks. 'Hall got ten holes in his aeroplane, and Kiffin and he got away by hiding in the clouds'.

Two days after Nungesser's success, Adjutant Bert Hall scored his second victory over a Fokker E III. Hall is shown beside his Nieuport 16, decorated with the name *BERT*, which was rendered in mirror image form on the other side of the fuselage (*H H Wynne*)

The events of 21 July seemed to spark a revival of N124's fortunes. On the 23rd Bert Hall was attacked by a Fokker E III that he described as being 'decorated up like a new saloon'. The German missed, dived under his Nieuport and came up in front of him. Hall got on his tail, followed him in a dive and fired two bursts. The Fokker rolled on its back and spun down to crash between Fort Vaux and Damloup.

On 27 July Lt de Laage de Meux opened his account with N124 by downing an Aviatik between Ornes and Bezonvaux for his second victory overall. On the 30th Sgt Lufbery sent a two-seater down to crash near Forêt d'Etain, possibly killing Obltn Oskar Illing and Hermann Kraft from *Kampfstaffel* 33 of *Kampfgeschwader* (KG) 6. His first instalment of revenge for Marc Pourpe entitled 'Luf' to a shot of Paul Rockwell's bourbon. He would eventually account for half the bottle, starting the next day, after downing a two-seater over Fort Vaux.

On 4 August Lufbery found himself teaming up with another future ace in Adjutant Victor Sayaret of N57 as they attacked and destroyed a two-seater over Abancourt, killing Uffz Peter Engel and Ltn Otto Maiwald of F. Fl. Abt. 34. It was the third confirmed victory for both pilots.

Four days later 'Luf' spotted a lone Aviatik south of Douaumont and carefully scanned the sky in accordance with what he had already made part of his tactical dicta – 'Always remember it may be a trap'. Satisfied that there were no other enemy aeroplanes around, he approached the two-seater from below and behind and emptied a Lewis drum into it. His fourth victim crashed in flames, killing Uffz Georg Gering and Ltn Max Sedlmair of *Kampfstaffel* 36, KG 6.

Lufbery was awarded the *Médaille Militaire* and *Croix de Guerre* with palm for his impressive string of successes. In addition to his mature

Sgt Raoul Lufbery stands alongside his Nieuport 11 N1256, bearing his monogram. After scoring his first victory on 30 July 1916, 'Luf' raised his score to four in less than two weeks, establishing himself as N124's deadliest pilot (*US Air Force Museum via Jon Guttman*)

Sgt Paul Pavelka's Nieuport 11 N1208 displays an unusual, non-standard camouflage pattern and monogram emblem, probably in red (*National Archives*)

approach to combat, Thenault took note of Lufbery's remarkable endurance, which allowed him to fly to altitudes of 18,000 ft three or four times a day without ill effect. In consequence, he usually assigned 'Luf' to fly high cover during patrols, 'to dominate the situation'.

As a former mechanic, Lufbery also continued to take a personal hand in keeping his aircraft in peak condition. A later squadron mate, Edward Hinkle, recalled that 'Anyone would rather have a secondhand Lufbery machine than a new one, anytime'.

On 11 August Sgt Paul Pavelka joined N124, but the Nieuport he received was the one in which Thaw had been wounded, and in which Prince had subsequently cracked up. In spite of having new wings and a

A close-up of Pavelka's Nieuport 16, seen from the other side, shows interesting details of the cockpit arrangement, the overwing machine gun mounting and the Lewis gun, with its ammunition drum removed (*National Archives*)

Nungesser sports his trademark *'Coeur Noir'* emblem on his shirt as well as on the side of his Nieuport 17 (*Jon Guttman*)

patched-up fuselage, the 'hoodooed machine' performed well during Pavelka's first familiarisation flight over the lines with de Laage and Rockwell.

However, two days later, while he was patrolling at 9000 ft over Verdun, the engine caught fire. Banking and side-slipping, Pavelka raced the flames to earth – and seemed to be losing, as the wing fabric caught fire. He managed to pull up just seconds before his aeroplane mushed into a swamp. Pavelka climbed from the cockpit and was sprinting for cover when the fuel tank exploded – after which German artillery, guided by the rising plume of smoke, fired on the wreck. Somehow surviving with nothing worse than singed eyebrows and slightly blistered hands, Pavelka was soon back in the air – with a new aeroplane.

On 15 August Nungesser terminated his affiliation with N124 and rejoined N65. In spite of more wounds and injuries, he would survive the war as France's third-ranking ace with 43 victories. Dissatisfied with barnstorming and stunt flying in the post-war world, Nungesser set out with navigator François Coli on 8 May 1927 in a specially modified Levasseur PL 8 in an attempt to fly the Atlantic Ocean from Paris to New York. They were never seen again.

Jimmy McConnell crashed while coming in from an evening patrol in late August, causing painful back injuries that he tried to dismiss, but which compelled Thenault to order him to the hospital at Vitry-le-François on the 26th. He spent most of a 45-day recuperation period at Mrs Weeks' apartment in Paris, writing a book about his experiences in N124 that was published on 20 February 1917 as *Flying For France*. Intended to counter the myths already circulating about the *escadrille*, and to stir up American sentiment for the French cause, it also showed McConnell to be a genuinely talented writer.

Meanwhile, a feud was simmering between Adjutant Prince and some of his squadronmates, especially Kiffin Rockwell, whose letters accused Prince of currying favour with Thenault at his comrades' expense. When Prince claimed a two-seater over Bois d'Hingry on 25 August, Thenault put him in for the *Médaille Militaire*, but in a 1 September letter to his brother, Rockwell wrote resentfully that nobody believed that he had actually scored it – 'in fact, everyone is sure he didn't'.

Bert Hall was also rubbing his squadronmates up the wrong way, both for his ungentlemanly language and his suspiciously consistent success in poker. Cheating one's comrades-in-arms is a serious charge, but even in a clean game Hall's experience in determining a man's hand from his facial expression must have given him a winning edge at a table full of relatively naive millionaires' sons. The others also applied Hall's penchant for telling tall tales to his character in general, with the exception of the equally worldly Lufbery, who once told Hall, 'I like a good yarn, true or not', and wryly remarked of Hall's ongoing diary, 'I'll bet that'll be a prime piece of hokum when it's finished'. Nevertheless, even Hall's harshest critic, N124 historian Paul Rockwell, admitted that he did good work for the unit, including the destruction of a photographic aeroplane northeast of Douaumont on 28 August.

The *Escadrille Americaine* concluded its operations over Verdun in fine style on 9 September, although ironically the day's successes involved two bitter antagonists. In one action, Prince teamed up with Lt Victor Regnier of N112 to down a Fokker over Fort Rozeiller. Elsewhere, Rockwell finally gained personal revenge for Chapman when he attacked a two-seater, hitting its observer with his first burst and pursuing it down to 4000 ft, before two intervening German fighters forced him to disengage. French ground observers subsequently confirmed the crash of Rockwell's second confirmed victory.

Rumsey's Nieuport 11 N1290 heads a N124 line-up at Behonne. The third machine from the right, with the white *X* marking on the fuselage, was Masson's (*National Archives*)

COLOUR PLATES

Artist, and World War 1 aficionado, Harry Dempsey has created the colour profiles for this volume, working closely with the author to portray the aircraft as accurately as circumstances permit. Some of the illustrations are, admittedly, reconstructions based on fragmentary photographic evidence or descriptions provided by the pilots while they were alive, combined with known unit marking policy. The colours portrayed are sometimes approximations, though the author is greatly indebted to Alan Toelle for his ground-breaking work in that field, which eliminated a lot of guesswork.

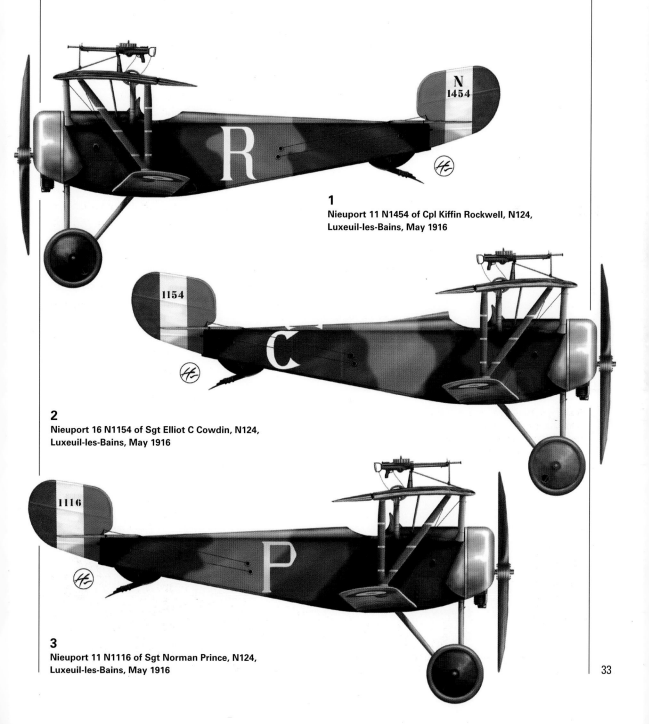

1
Nieuport 11 N1454 of Cpl Kiffin Rockwell, N124, Luxeuil-les-Bains, May 1916

2
Nieuport 16 N1154 of Sgt Elliot C Cowdin, N124, Luxeuil-les-Bains, May 1916

3
Nieuport 11 N1116 of Sgt Norman Prince, N124, Luxeuil-les-Bains, May 1916

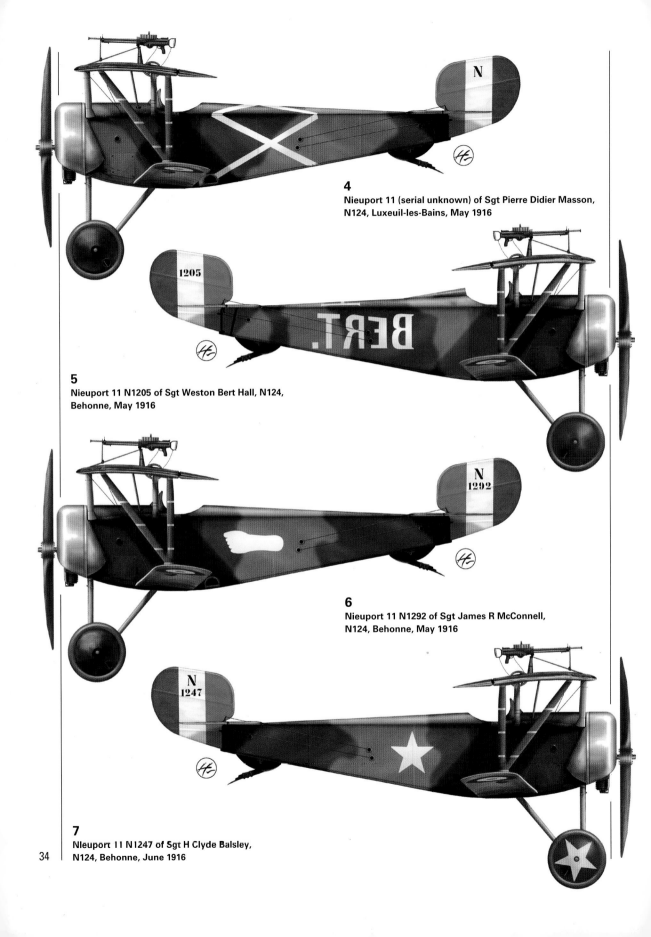

4
Nieuport 11 (serial unknown) of Sgt Pierre Didier Masson,
N124, Luxeuil-les-Bains, May 1916

5
Nieuport 11 N1205 of Sgt Weston Bert Hall, N124,
Behonne, May 1916

6
Nieuport 11 N1292 of Sgt James R McConnell,
N124, Behonne, May 1916

7
Nieuport 11 N1247 of Sgt H Clyde Balsley,
N124, Behonne, June 1916

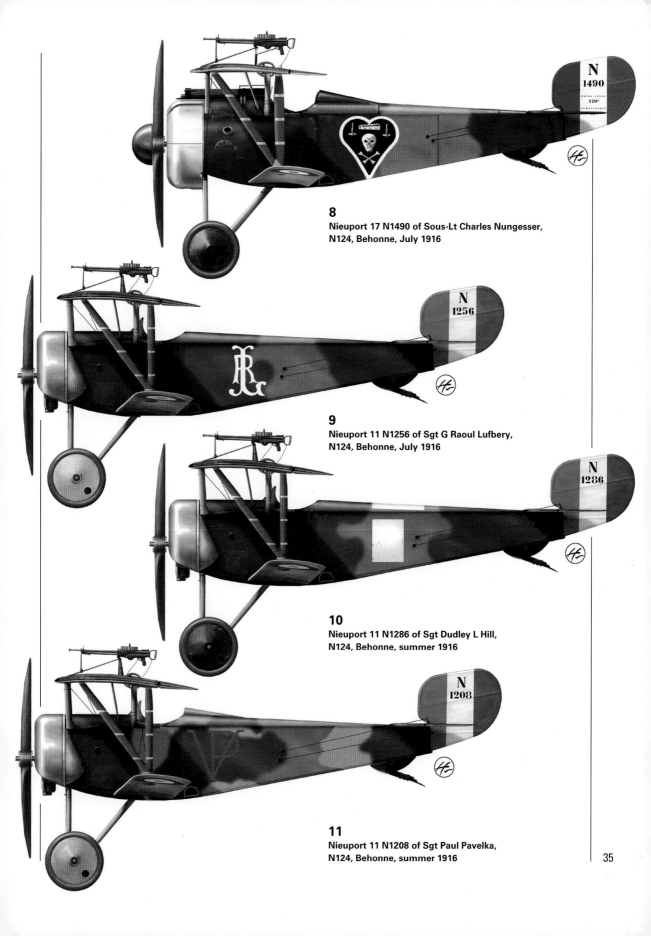

8
Nieuport 17 N1490 of Sous-Lt Charles Nungesser,
N124, Behonne, July 1916

9
Nieuport 11 N1256 of Sgt G Raoul Lufbery,
N124, Behonne, July 1916

10
Nieuport 11 N1286 of Sgt Dudley L Hill,
N124, Behonne, summer 1916

11
Nieuport 11 N1208 of Sgt Paul Pavelka,
N124, Behonne, summer 1916

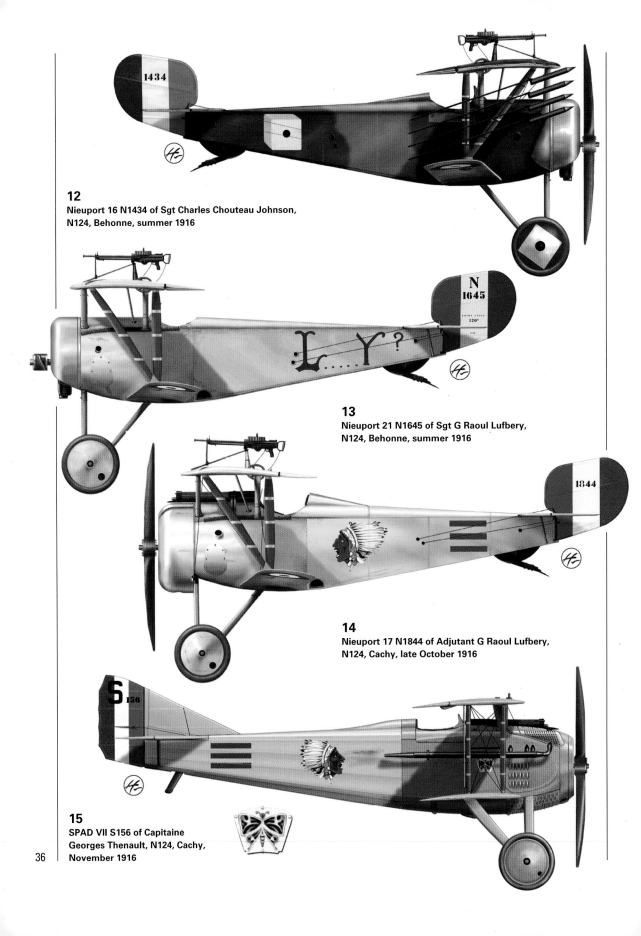

12
Nieuport 16 N1434 of Sgt Charles Chouteau Johnson,
N124, Behonne, summer 1916

13
Nieuport 21 N1645 of Sgt G Raoul Lufbery,
N124, Behonne, summer 1916

14
Nieuport 17 N1844 of Adjutant G Raoul Lufbery,
N124, Cachy, late October 1916

15
SPAD VII S156 of Capitaine
Georges Thenault, N124, Cachy,
November 1916

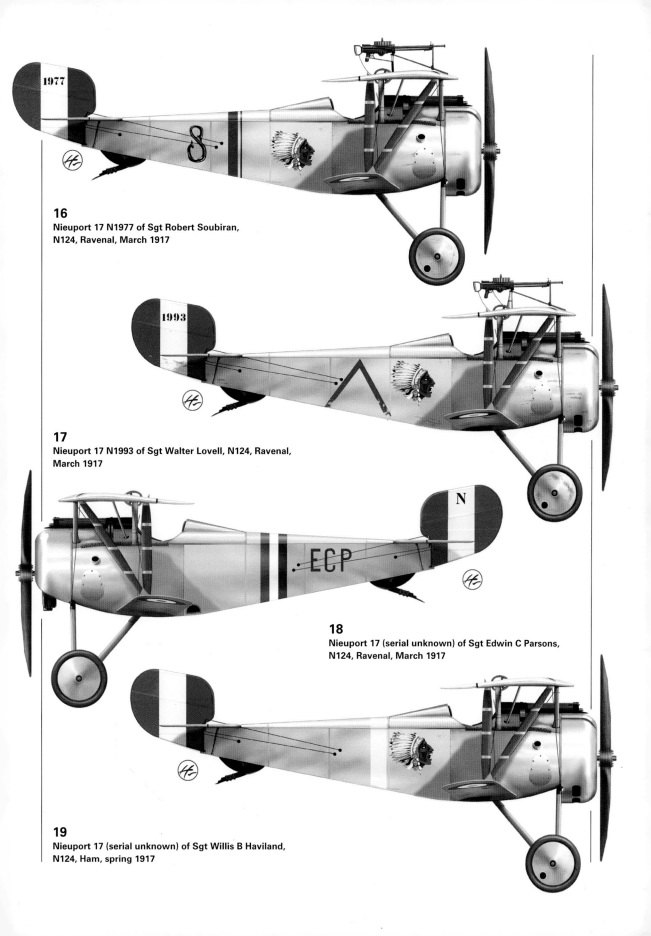

16
Nieuport 17 N1977 of Sgt Robert Soubiran,
N124, Ravenal, March 1917

17
Nieuport 17 N1993 of Sgt Walter Lovell, N124, Ravenal,
March 1917

18
Nieuport 17 (serial unknown) of Sgt Edwin C Parsons,
N124, Ravenal, March 1917

19
Nieuport 17 (serial unknown) of Sgt Willis B Haviland,
N124, Ham, spring 1917

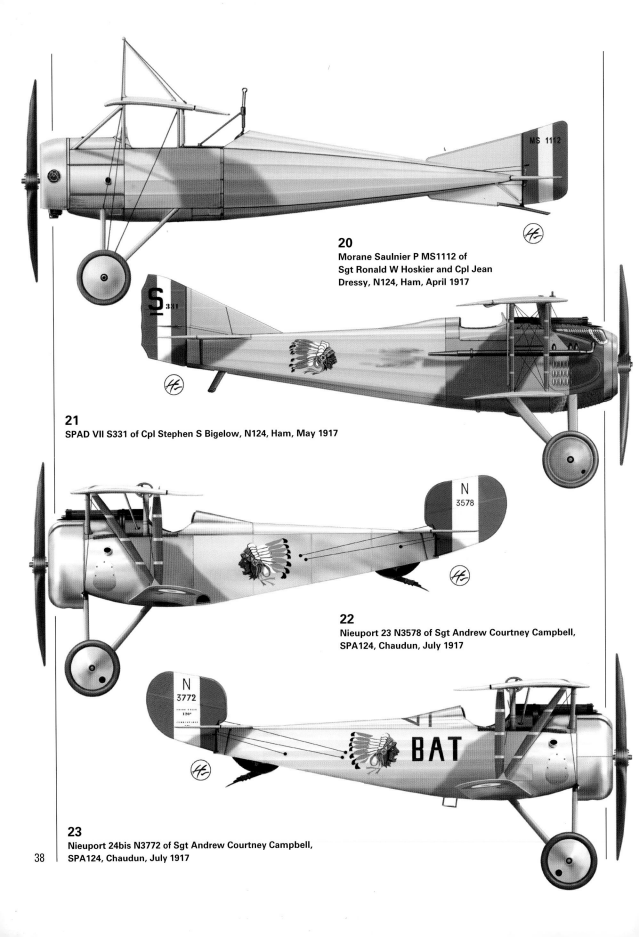

20
Morane Saulnier P MS1112 of
Sgt Ronald W Hoskier and Cpl Jean
Dressy, N124, Ham, April 1917

21
SPAD VII S331 of Cpl Stephen S Bigelow, N124, Ham, May 1917

22
Nieuport 23 N3578 of Sgt Andrew Courtney Campbell,
SPA124, Chaudun, July 1917

23
Nieuport 24bis N3772 of Sgt Andrew Courtney Campbell,
SPA124, Chaudun, July 1917

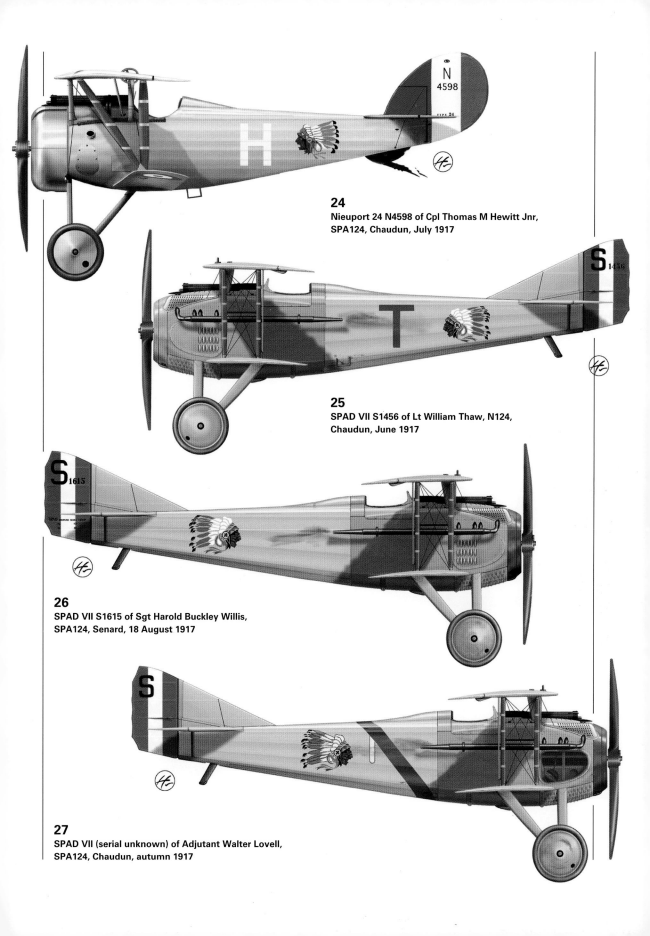

24
Nieuport 24 N4598 of Cpl Thomas M Hewitt Jnr,
SPA124, Chaudun, July 1917

25
SPAD VII S1456 of Lt William Thaw, N124,
Chaudun, June 1917

26
SPAD VII S1615 of Sgt Harold Buckley Willis,
SPA124, Senard, 18 August 1917

27
SPAD VII (serial unknown) of Adjutant Walter Lovell,
SPA124, Chaudun, autumn 1917

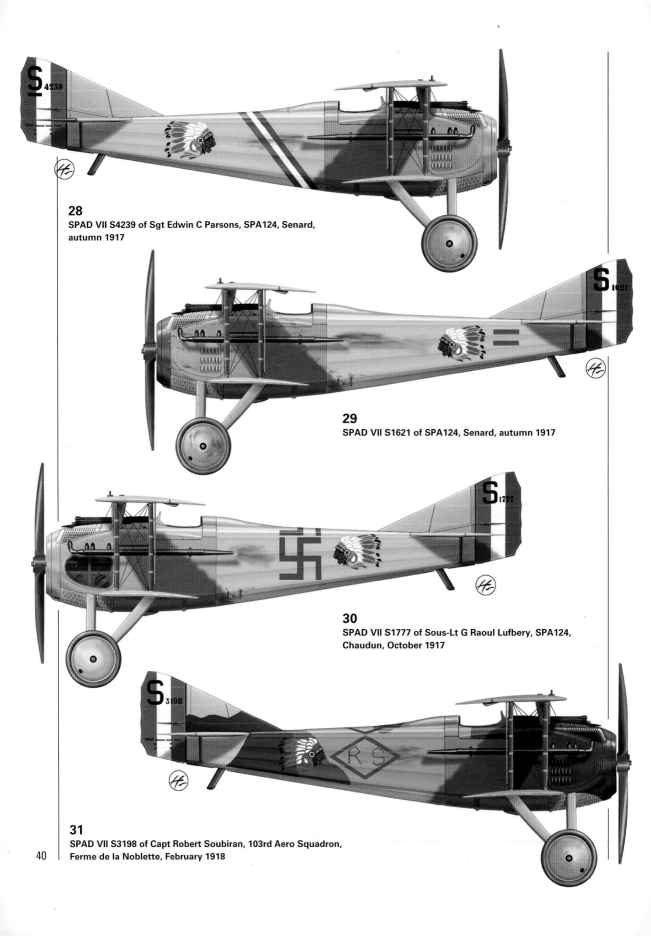

28
SPAD VII S4239 of Sgt Edwin C Parsons, SPA124, Senard,
autumn 1917

29
SPAD VII S1621 of SPA124, Senard, autumn 1917

30
SPAD VII S1777 of Sous-Lt G Raoul Lufbery, SPA124,
Chaudun, October 1917

31
SPAD VII S3198 of Capt Robert Soubiran, 103rd Aero Squadron,
Ferme de la Noblette, February 1918

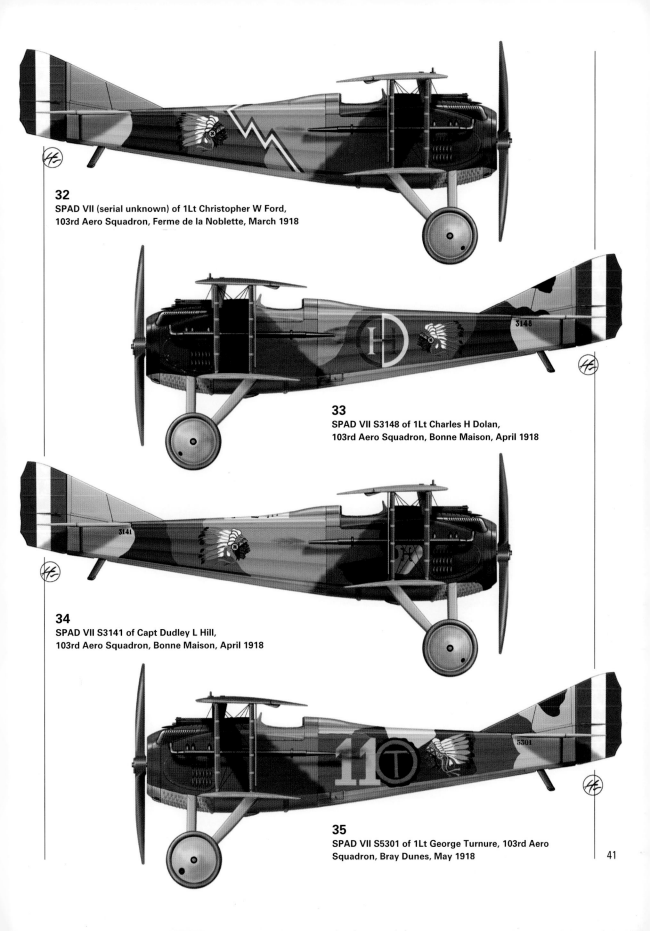

32
SPAD VII (serial unknown) of 1Lt Christopher W Ford,
103rd Aero Squadron, Ferme de la Noblette, March 1918

33
SPAD VII S3148 of 1Lt Charles H Dolan,
103rd Aero Squadron, Bonne Maison, April 1918

34
SPAD VII S3141 of Capt Dudley L Hill,
103rd Aero Squadron, Bonne Maison, April 1918

35
SPAD VII S5301 of 1Lt George Turnure, 103rd Aero
Squadron, Bray Dunes, May 1918

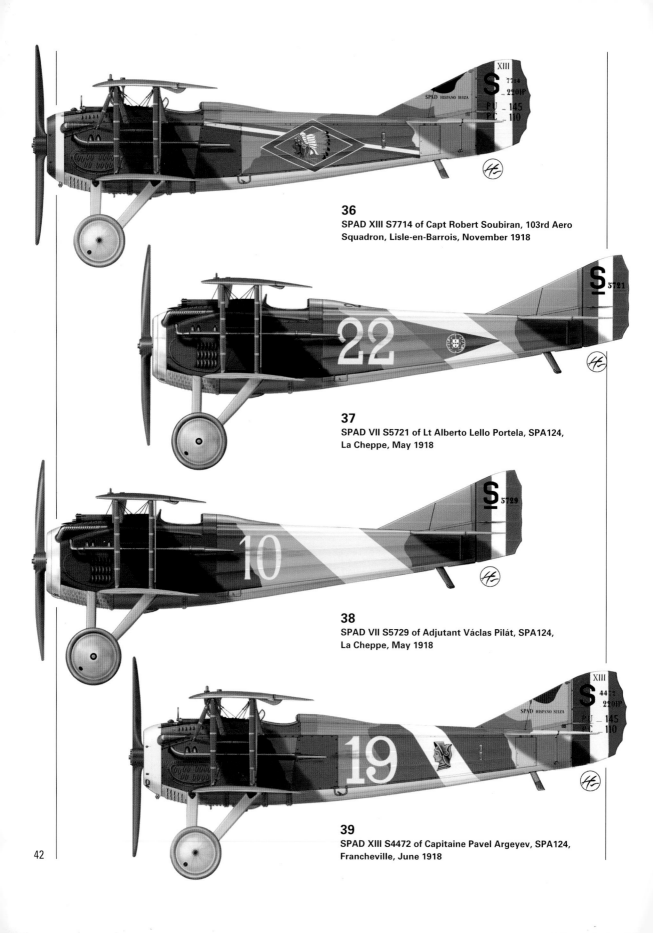

36
SPAD XIII S7714 of Capt Robert Soubiran, 103rd Aero
Squadron, Lisle-en-Barrois, November 1918

37
SPAD VII S5721 of Lt Alberto Lello Portela, SPA124,
La Cheppe, May 1918

38
SPAD VII S5729 of Adjutant Václas Pilát, SPA124,
La Cheppe, May 1918

39
SPAD XIII S4472 of Capitaine Pavel Argeyev, SPA124,
Francheville, June 1918

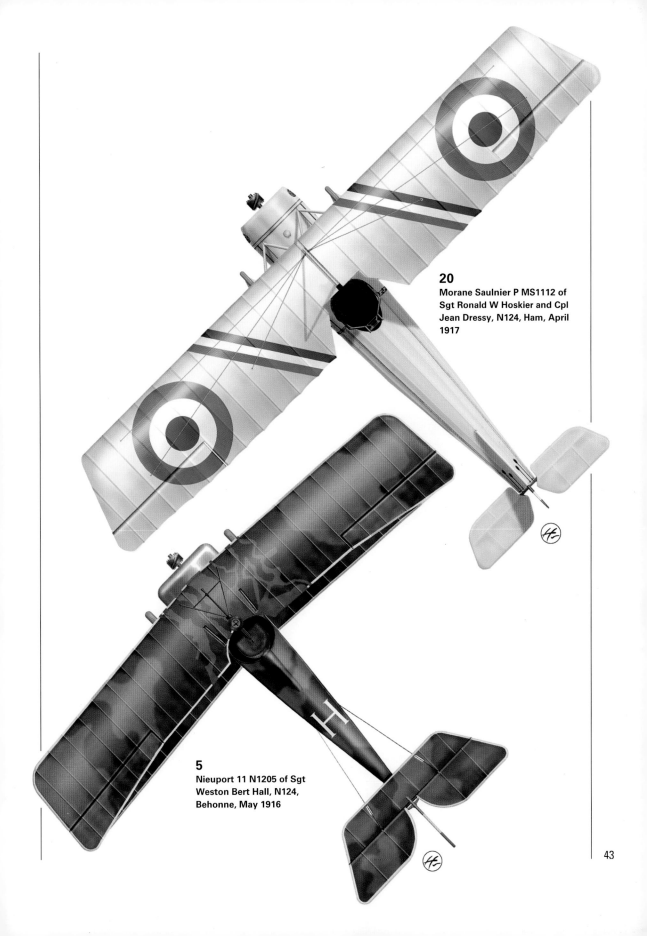

20
Morane Saulnier P MS1112 of
Sgt Ronald W Hoskier and Cpl
Jean Dressy, N124, Ham, April
1917

5
Nieuport 11 N1205 of Sgt
Weston Bert Hall, N124,
Behonne, May 1916

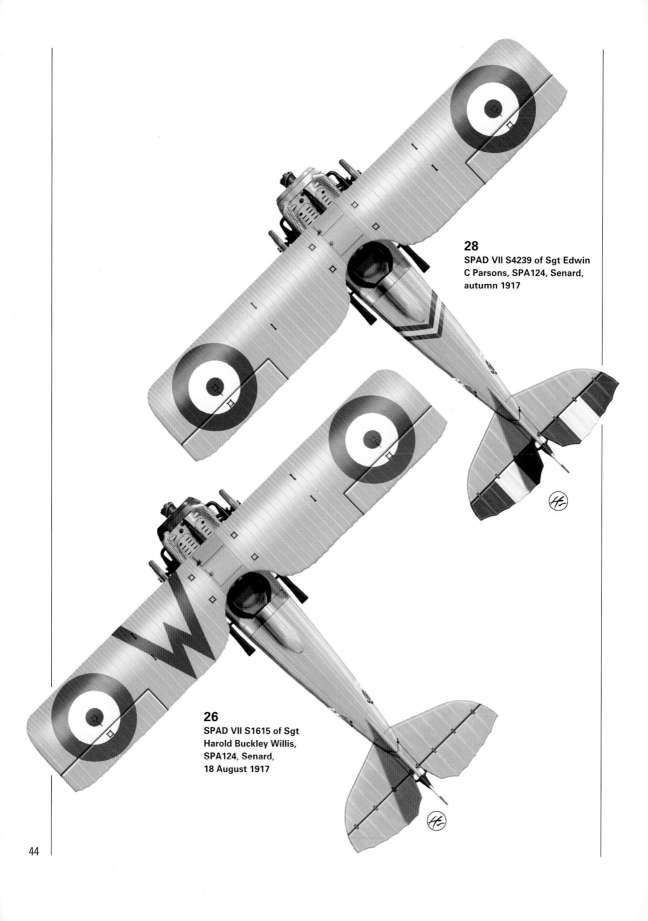

28
SPAD VII S4239 of Sgt Edwin
C Parsons, SPA124, Senard,
autumn 1917

26
SPAD VII S1615 of Sgt
Harold Buckley Willis,
SPA124, Senard,
18 August 1917

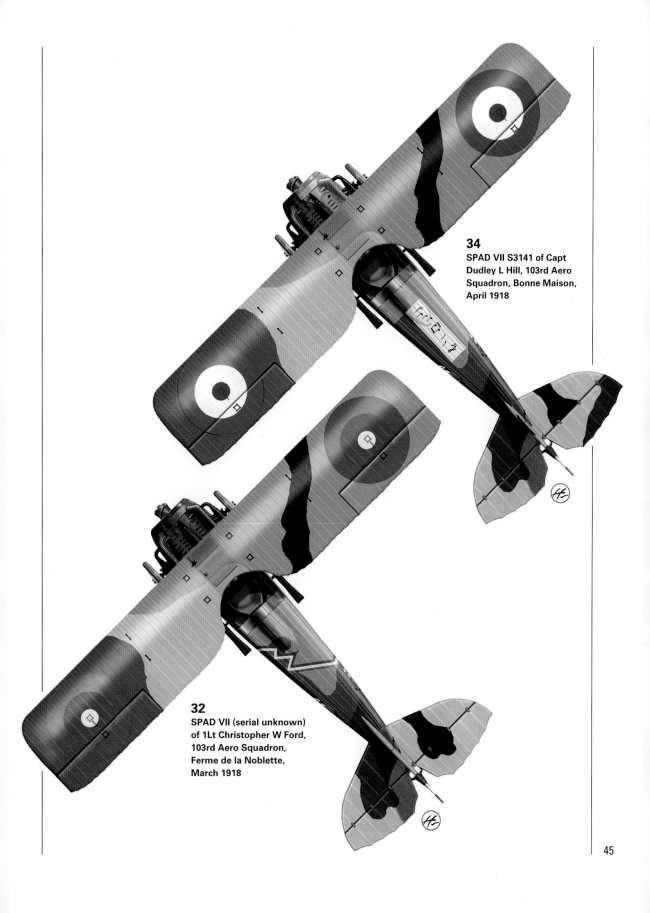

34
SPAD VII S3141 of Capt
Dudley L Hill, 103rd Aero
Squadron, Bonne Maison,
April 1918

32
SPAD VII (serial unknown)
of 1Lt Christopher W Ford,
103rd Aero Squadron,
Ferme de la Noblette,
March 1918

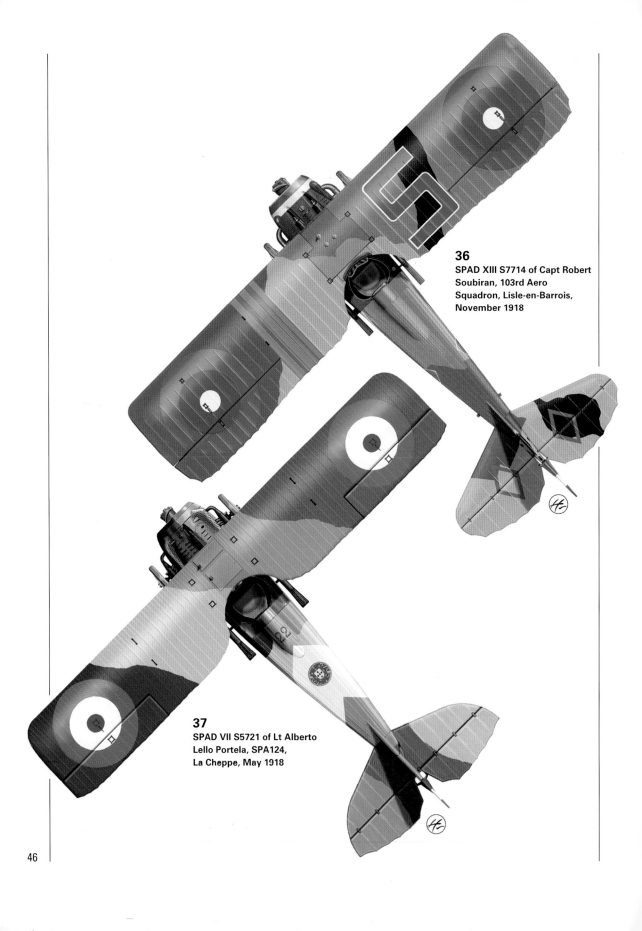

36
SPAD XIII S7714 of Capt Robert
Soubiran, 103rd Aero
Squadron, Lisle-en-Barrois,
November 1918

37
SPAD VII S5721 of Lt Alberto
Lello Portela, SPA124,
La Cheppe, May 1918

THE OBERNDORF RAID

On 14 September 1916 N124 was ordered back to Luxeuil to support Happe's bombers. During its time at Behonne, the *escadrille* had fought 146 combats and been credited with 13 victories, for the loss of one pilot killed and three wounded. Before leaving Bar-le-Duc, the Americans turned their worn-out Nieuport 11s over to another *escadrille*, and on 19 September they began receiving Nieuport 17s, which were redesigned to provide a better-balanced airframe for the 110-hp Le Rhône engine than the Nieuport 16 had afforded, as well as mounting a synchronised 0.30-cal Vickers machine gun.

While en route to Luxeuil, the Americans enjoyed a three-day stay in Paris, during which Robert Rockwell joined the unit. Born in Cincinnati, Ohio, on 19 March 1892, Robert Locherbie Rockwell was the son of a railroad executive who had studied at Howe Military School in Indiana, Kenyon College in Ohio, and at the College of Physicians and Surgeons at New York University, before joining the Anglo-American Ambulance Service in early 1915. A distant cousin of Paul and Kiffin Rockwell, he decided to follow the latter into aviation, training at Buc and Pau

Another new arrival at N124 in September 1916 was Whiskey, a lion cub purchased in Paris, shown with Kiffin Rockwell, Bill Thaw and Paul Pavelka (*Jon Guttman*)

alongside a new generation of N124 members – Willis Haviland, Fred Prince and Robert Soubiran. Chosen by Thenault on 17 September, he soon acquired the nickname 'Doc' for his training in medicine.

Rockwell was not the only new squadron member that N124 acquired while in Paris. While reading the Paris edition of the *New York Herald*, Dudley Hill found a classified advertisement placed by a Brazilian dentist for a four-month-old lion cub that he had bought to entertain his clients, but which was now unnerving them. Deciding that the animal would make an ideal mascot, Hill, Hall, Johnson, Prince, Rockwell and Thaw pooled their money to meet the dentist's asking price of 500 francs.

Although their new pet forced them to change hotels frequently, and Thaw had to have a wooden cage made so his 'African dog' could travel in the luggage car of their train, the Americans eventually got him to Luxeuil, where he acquired a taste for a saucer-full of whiskey, and was christened accordingly. Pampered by the squadron, Whiskey soon became friendly with all its personnel, as well as Fram and the other canines. He seldom bit or scratched, but his penchant for gnawing on anything within reach – usually dress uniforms or the decorations on them – frequently caused consternation, amusement, or both.

At Luxeuil, Capitaine Happe had been commanding *Groupe de Bombardement* 4 in operations against German industrial targets when another bombing unit joined him early in June 1916 – 3 Wing, Royal Naval Air Service (RNAS). Formed largely in response to German Zeppelin raids on England, 3 Wing was equipped with Sopwith 1½ Strutters, in the form of both single-seat bombers and two-seat fighters to escort them.

The wing's first mission on 30 July 1916 involved three Sopwiths joining six French bombers of GB4 on an attack on Mülheim. Some of the wing's aircraft were transferred to support the Battle of the Somme soon afterwards, however, and by the autumn 3 Wing had to fill out its strength with lumbering Breguet-Michelin V pushers purchased from the French.

In September 1916, Nieuport 17s began arriving at N124. Powered by the same 110-hp Le Rhône engine as the Nieuport 16, the new French scout had a redesigned fuselage and an increased, 15-square-metre wing area that made it much easier to fly than its notoriously tricky predecessor. Nieuport 17 N1582 was assigned to Lt Thaw (*National Archives*)

A visiting US Army officer examines Lufbery's Nieuport 21 N1615. A variant of the Nieuport 17 powered by an 80-hp Le Rhône engine, the Nieuport 21 was generally used as a fighter trainer only (*National Archives*)

Sgt Kiffin Rockwell beside his Nieuport 17 in September 1916. Rockwell was killed in action on 23 September, soon after N124's return to Luxeuil-les-Bains (*SHAA B76.872*)

By August 1916, four *groupes de bombardement* were striking at targets such as Ludwigshafen, Mannheim, Pechebronn and Dillingen in the heavily industrialised Saar Valley and even the Rhine. As aerial opposition increased, Happe developed a V-shaped formation to concentrate defensive fire against the Fokker and Pfalz Eindeckers that had been intercepting the bomber formations since mid-1915. Part of N124's job was to deal with those German fighters.

The resumption of operations from Luxeuil got off to a heartbreaking start. On 23 September, just three days after his 24th birthday, Kiffin Rockwell joined Lufbery on a morning sortie to engage some Fokkers that had been sighted flying between Colmar and Habsheim. Soon after take-off, Lufbery experienced trouble with his Vickers gun and landed at Fontaine to readjust its synchronisation gear.

Rockwell chose to continue the mission alone, and over Rodern he spotted an Albatros two-seater 11,000 ft below him, heading toward Allied lines. The German observer fired at long range and Rockwell, as usual, dived directly on the enemy, holding his fire until a mid-air collision was imminent. This time, however, it was the German who struck home first – ground observers saw Rockwell's Nieuport (No 1811) falter, then fall to earth, shedding a wing before crashing in a field of flowers. French soldiers found a gaping wound from a disintegrating bullet in his chest.

As field telephones spread the news of Rockwell's death, a vengeful Lufbery took off from Fontaine and hovered over Habsheim aerodrome, trying to bait German aircraft to come up, but none accepted the challenge.

Although he had asked Pavelka to be buried wherever he fell on the very night before he died, Rockwell was ceremoniously buried at Luxeuil, with aeroplanes circling above and dropping flowers on his French flag-draped coffin. The French posthumously commissioned him a sous-lieutenant and made him a *Chevalier de la Légion d'Honneur*. For many members of N124 it was all poor consolation. 'No greater blow could have befallen the *escadrille*', McConnell wrote. 'Kiffin was its soul'.

Thaw stands beside N1582, which was an early Nieuport 17 that featured a non-rotating *'cône de pénétration'* in front of the propeller. By that time Thaw was identifying his aircraft with the initial of his surname, and he would continue to do so until May 1918 (*National Archives*)

If one really could believe that the deaths of Chapman and Rockwell and the injuring of Thaw had torn out N124's soul, it still retained a calculating brain in the person of Lufbery, who was promoted to adjutant on the 26th. Even 'Luf' learned that he was not invincible, however, when he engaged what he called 'a big white two-seater of very substantial appearance' on 9 October. Typically, he dived from above but attacked from below, only to find the alert observer ready and waiting. Lufbery's engine was hit and he had to glide home.

When he examined his Nieuport, he found his cowling full of holes and the engine demolished, several holes in his fuel tank, his left aileron shot away and one of his interplane struts splintered. In addition, his left flying boot was ripped open and another bullet had entered his flying suit and grazed his chest.

On the same day that Lufbery was promoted, Prince received the *Médaille Militaire*. On 10 October, the day following 'Luf's' close call, Prince had one of his own when he engaged some Fokkers over Altkirch and shot one down, probably killing Uffz Julius Heck of KEK 5. Prince returned with his Nieuport riddled, proving that whatever doubts Rockwell may have had of his self-serving nature, he was not lacking in courage or, on this occasion at least, veracity.

On 12 October, four members of N124 took part in the most epic mission involving their squadron since its inception when they escorted a remarkable Anglo-French bombing raid against the Mauser arms factory at Oberndorf-am-Neckar, which lay 175 kilometres from Luxeuil. Happe had received the order to attack the plant on 8 September, but the operation had to wait until his squadrons could obtain replacements for their worn-out aircraft – including licence-built Sopwiths. In early October Happe judged his units ready to mount an effective effort, and laid plans for a joint operation.

GB4 was then comprised of F29, F123 and BM120. F123's Farman 40 and 42 bombers were supplemented by 12 new Sopwiths, but only one of the latter would escort them to the target on the actual mission. Escort for BM120's Breguets would be provided by four Nieuport 17s from N124, with Lt de Laage leading Lufbery, Masson and Prince. The bombers would be aloft for five hours – more than double the duration of their Nieuport escorts – so the four fighters had to fly ahead and land at an advance airfield at Corcieux to refuel before proceeding to the target. They would stop at Corcieux again on the return flight to Luxeuil.

Also participating in the raid would be two flights each of single-seat Sopwith bombers from Blue and Red squadrons of 3 Wing, with seven Sopwith two-seaters serving as escorts. In addition to the total of 62 aircraft slated to bomb Oberndorf, 18 Caudron G4s of C61 were to mount a diversionary raid on Lörrach to the south – only four actually carried out the mission.

Dense cloud cover over the Black Forest further delayed the Oberndorf strike, but just after noon on 12 October a reconnaissance aeroplane reported weather favourable enough to permit a sortie. Between 1315 and 1340 hrs, six Farmans of F29 and six of F123 took off, followed at 1345 hrs by seven Breguet IVs of BM120 and one Breguet V seconded to that unit from the British. Two Farmans apiece from F29 and F123 reversed course with mechanical problems, and a fifth F123 aeroplane, struck by anti-aircraft fire, turned back and force-landed in Allied territory in the Vosges Mountains.

A pioneer hero of French aerial bombing, Capitaine Maurice Happe led one of the largest raids of 1916 against the Mauser factory at Oberndorf on 12 October, with four members of N124 flying as escort (*Jon Guttman*)

This Breguet-Michelin BM IV was flown by Lt Lemaître, commander of BM120, during the Oberndorf raid. N124's primary mission was to escort his bombers to and from the target (*SHAA B83.3698*)

At 1340 hrs, the first of 26 Sopwiths and Breguets from 3 Wing began taking off. One of the Sopwith two-seaters was flown by the wing's commander, Richard Bell-Davies, who had received the Victoria Cross for rescuing a downed comrade in Bulgaria on 19 November 1915. Three Sopwith bombers and one fighter had to turn back with engine trouble, and a fifth bomber crashed at Faucogney 25 minutes after take-off.

Astride the raiders' route lay the German aerodrome at Colmar-Nord, from which *Bayerische Fliegerabteilung* (Bavarian Flying Detachment) 9, or F. Fl. Abt. 9b, operated six Ago C I two-seat, twin-boom pusher biplanes, with a small fighter component – KEK Ensisheim – based south of that aerodrome. Farther south, at Habsheim near Mülhausen, were F. Fl. Abt. 48 and a unit equipped with Fokker E III and D II fighters, originally dubbed KEK Habsheim, but recently redesignated *Jagdstaffel* or *Jasta* 15.

At 1504 hrs the operations room at Colmar received a telephone call that five enemy aeroplanes were flying east from Gebweiler. Suspecting its own aerodrome to be the target, F. Fl. Abt. 9b scrambled up all of its aeroplanes, including three Fokker D IIs from KEK Ensisheim, flown by Ltn Otto Kissenberth and Vzfw Ludwig Hanstein and Ludwig Hilz. Meanwhile, a confusing succession of new reports followed: seven enemy aeroplanes coming from Hilsenfirst to the east; 12 from Gebweiler to Ensisheim; five from Ensisheim to Neuf Breisach; ten from Buchenkopf to the southeast; 15 from Thann to the northeast.

Happe's four Farmans of F29, in the vanguard of the aerial procession, surprised the German defences, dropped their bombs on Oberndorf unopposed and returning to Luxeuil safely, with one of his crews claiming

Ltn Otto Kissenberth of *Kampfeinsitzer Kommando* Habsheim flies a mission in the Fokker D II in which he opposed the bombers attacking Oberndorf (*Greg VanWyngarden*)

a Fokker over the target area. However, as F123's three Farmans flew over the great forest between Neuf Breisach and Colmar, they were stalked from behind by Kissenberth and Hilz. Kissenberth was first to score, sending the leading Farman down into the woods near Bidensolen, where its exploding bombs threw a funeral pyre 100 metres into the air for its crew, Adjutant Henri Baron and Sgt André Guerineau.

Unaware of their comrades' fate because of the flak exploding around them, Sous-Lt Armand Georges and Sgt Ernest Jouan flew on until Kissenberth caught up with them over Ihringen and opened fire. The Farman fell over on one wing and crashed near the Breisach-Freiburg railway line. Out of ammunition and almost out of fuel, Kissenberth landed at Flugpark Neuf Breisach and phoned in his first combat report.

It is possible that Kissenberth's retirement was misinterpreted by other F123 crews as indicating that he was in trouble – Brigadier Jean Pierre de Gaillard de la Valdène and Cpl Pichon, flying F123's Sopwith escort aeroplane, was credited with what Gaillard described as 'an altogether small two-seater biplane of a type absolutely new', which dived on his tail before being shot down. Gaillard's description also suggests that his opponent may have been a Fokker D II of *Jasta* 15 that had been modified by its pilot, Vfw Ernst Udet, with a dummy gunner made of sheet metal, mounted behind his cockpit to keep enemy aeroplanes off his tail. In any event, Udet was not shot down, as BM120 would soon discover.

Red Squadron of 3 Wing bombed Oberndorf, but as its nine Sopwiths turned for home they came under attack by German fighters, including Kissenberth and Hilz, who had taken off again after replenishing their fuel and ammunition. Kissenberth engaged a two-seater Sopwith that put up a spirited fight until its ammunition was expended. The Sopwith's engine was damaged, but its Canadian pilot, Flt Sub-Lt Raymond Collishaw, managed to limp back to Luxeuil.

Kissenberth landed at Freiburg, where he was joined by two other aircraft – Vfw Hanstein's Fokker and a Sopwith! Hanstein had wounded its British pilot, Flt Sub-Lt Charles H S Butterworth, in the neck and then driven him down in tight circles until he landed on the parade field outside Freiburg. As he landed, Hanstein's scalp was creased by a bullet – fired by trigger-happy mechanics from the nearby Gotha *Geschwaderschule*.

Red Squadron's remaining eight Sopwiths returned safely, but the worst aerial carnage of the mission lay in store for the eight Breguets of BM120. Things began on a fairly encouraging note. While waiting to rendezvous with BM120's oncoming aeroplanes, N124's pilots spotted

Also opposing the Oberndorf raiders was Vzfw Ernst Udet of *Jagdstaffel* 15, flying this Fokker D III complete with a dummy gunner mounted behind the cockpit! (*Greg VanWyngarden*)

Germans examine the Breguet-Michelin BM IV brought down by Udet during the Oberndorf raid – with all its bombs still on the racks! It was the second of an eventual 62 victories for Germany's future second-ranking World War 1 ace (*Charles Donald Collection via Jon Guttman*)

four Fokker E IIIs lying in wait north of Colmar and immediately engaged them, one being credited to Prince. With N124 guarding their flanks, the bombers flew on, but as they emerged from the Vosges, to the southwest, *Jasta* 15 scrambled several fighters to intercept them. Among the Germans was Ernst Udet, who wrote of the action after the war;

'Because it flew directly under me, it was easy work. I dropped down past the Nieuports, placed myself in a safe position behind the leading machine and, with 350 shots, forced it to land. It landed intact, and in order to prevent the occupants from destroying it, I landed beside it. Because my tyres were punctured by shots, I turned over, but without serious consequences. It was a comical picture; the vanquished landed upright and the victor landed upside-down. Both Frenchmen clambered down and we shook hands all around.'

Udet's victim was a Breguet IV marked with a black and white chequered square on the nacelle and the ironic legend, *Le Voilá le Foudroyant* ('Here comes the thunderer'). After making a dead-stick landing at Rüstenhart with all their bombs still on the racks, Cpl Lucien Barlet and Soldat Luneau were elated to be alive, even if they would spend the next two years PoWs.

Three of F. Fl. Abt. 9b's Ago C Is tried to intercept the bombers over Freiburg, but F29 and F123 had already passed over that city by the time they arrived. Ltn Kiliani then directed his pilot, Ltn Hans Hartl, to turn west. The Agos flew over Münster and Schlossberg, made a wide turn near Rosskopf and ran right into BM120, which had just lost its first aircraft to Udet. Kiliani and Hartl joined *Jasta* 15 pilot Ltn Otto Pfältzer in forcing down another Breguet near Bremgarten.

Upon landing nearby, Kiliani tried to cut some tricoloured fabric from the bomber as a souvenir, but its crew, Sgt Nöel Bouet and Cpl Delcroix, warned him off, stating that they had already set their aeroplane on fire. Shortly afterward, the Breguet was destroyed as its bombs went off. Amid the confusion of the running fight, Ago crew Ltn Pfleiderer and Simson found themselves under attack by an Aviatik two-seater from F. Fl. Abt. 48, which fortunately caused no damage before its crew realised its error and peeled off.

Hilz, who joined the melée, singled out a Breguet from the formation and sent it down in flames over Umkirch, west of Freiburg, killing Cpl Robert de Montais and Soldat André Haas. Ago C I crew Vfw Ertl and Ltn Biedermann engaged another Breguet in a running fight along the length of the Elzacher Valley until Biedermann's machine gun ran out of ammunition. The bomber's crew was probably Cpls Tanner and Viaris de

The most remarkable feat among the N124 pilots during the Oberndorf raid was performed by Didier Masson, who was credited with downing a Fokker while his engine was dead, then gliding his Nieuport 17 back to Allied lines (*Greg Van Wyngarden*)

Lesogne, who reported being 'violently attacked by a twin-fuselage enemy' near Emmendingen, detached from the formation and closely pursued. Nevertheless, they survived, and Happe credited them with bringing down an Aviatik.

N124 had hardly been idle during the fight, with Didier Masson firing 50 rounds at an Aviatik and then turning on a Fokker. Just as he was about to fire, however, his engine sputtered to a halt – his fuel tank had been punctured. Figuring that he had just enough altitude to glide back to Allied territory, Masson turned for home, but his intended victim was soon on his tail, shooting up his upper wing and fuselage, windscreen and instrument panel. Becoming careless, however, the German came on too fast and zoomed under Masson's Nieuport.

Finding the enemy just below his nose, Masson banked and emptied his machine gun into the Fokker, which spun earthward until he lost sight of it one mile west of Neuf Briesach. Resuming his glide, Masson cleared the Rhine, passing so low over the lines that German infantry almost shot him down and his wheels almost snagged the French barbed wire, before coming to rest in a shell hole. Knowing what would happen next, Masson wasted no time in getting away from his aeroplane before German artillery demolished it.

The running fight continued to the target area, where the Breguets, now down to four, released their bombs and turned for home. During the return flight Lufbery was credited with shooting down a Roland C II over Schlettstadt. De Laage fired at a Fokker that was attacking a Breguet at the rear of the formation, but he did not feel sure enough of the outcome to request a confirmation.

The engine of the Breguet flown by Maréchal-des-Logis Léon Mottay and Cpl Marchand quit, and although they tried to glide their heavy machine to the Rhine, they were finally forced to land near Steinbach, only to crash at the Haslach-Offenburg railway. Marchand was killed and the injured Mottay was taken prisoner. They were probably the fifth accredited victory of Ltn Kurt Haber of *Jasta* 15.

Elsewhere, Davies led Blue Squadron's Breguets through heavy anti-aircraft fire and drove off some German aircraft that made a series of desultory attacks on his tight formation. 'We cleared the Black Forest and presently a small town appeared ahead', Davies reported. 'It did not look like Oberndorf, but the bombers seemed quite sure it was. They got into a single line and went down to bomb'.

As the returning British bombers crossed the Rhine Valley at sunset, Davies saw one of the Breguets go down. Although he saw no enemy aeroplanes involved, the Germans reported that Pfleiderer and Simson, while flying toward Colmar, encountered a homeward-bound Breguet and fired into its nacelle. At that point they were joined by Kissenberth's Fokker D II, which came up from behind to get a burst into the Breguet's motor. The gunner shot away one of Kissenberth's interplane struts, but his wing held up and he attacked again, sending bullets into the Breguet's cowling, while Simson hit its gunner from below. The bomber came down near Oberenzen, and Pfleiderer and Simson landed to take pilot Flt Sub-Lt Rockey and his badly wounded bombardier, Gunlayer Sturdee, prisoners.

Rather than press his luck any further, Kissenberth flew his damaged aeroplane back to Colmar-Nord, where he was also credited with the bomber's destruction – his third for the day. Another British Breguet V was brought down over Buggingen by flak, its pilot, Flt Sub-Lt Newman becoming a PoW and Gunlayer Vitty being mortally wounded.

The last German attack did not put an end to Allied losses, as damaged aeroplanes and wounded crews straggled back toward Luxeuil. The only F123 Farman that actually bombed Oberndorf crash-landed in the Vosges, injuring its pilot, Cpl Henri Tondu. The three remaining Breguets of BM120, unable to find their way in the darkness, managed to find some flat country to the northwest and landed successfully. One of 3 Wing's Breguets crashed at Buc and a Sopwith was similarly wrecked at Corbenay, but the British reported no crew casualties.

By the time N124 returned to Corcieux, it was so dark that oil fires had to be lit on the field to guide its Nieuports down. Lufbery's aeroplane bounced to a safe landing, but as Prince followed him in at a slightly lower altitude, his landing gear caught on a utility cable and crashed, throwing him from the cockpit. Prince tried to stand, but both of his legs were broken and he had suffered internal injuries.

What had been accomplished for the loss of 15 aircraft and 21 airmen? The Allies initially claimed to have dropped four tons of bombs on the Mauser plant and shot down six German aircraft. The Germans reported that 60 bombs fell on or around Oberndorf, killing three people and injuring seven, but that no significant damage was done and work at the Mauser plant had not been interrupted. 'No German machine was lost', their report concluded, 'and no aeronaut was killed or wounded in the action'. That was a slight exaggeration, for Uffz August Büchner of F. Fl. Abt. 6b was severely wounded that day.

Later intelligence reports confirmed Davies' suspicions – his six Breguets had bombed Donaueschingen, rather than Oberndorf.

Analysing lessons learned from the raid, the French concluded;

'(1) The bad quality of the aeroplanes or engines on the series F XLII (130-hp Renault engine).

'(2) The difficulty for the Sopwith aeroplanes to get a proper formation in the clouds.

Sgt Lufbery with Nieuport 17 N1803, which was probably the regular machine of Lt Thaw. 'Luf' was credited with a Roland C II over Oberndorf, making him the first ace of N124, and of the United States (*SHAA B85.1174*)

Ltn Kissenberth poses with the Breguet-Michelin BM V of 3 Wing, RNAS that he brought down for his third victory of the Oberndorf raid (*Greg VanWyngarden*)

'Finally, other long distance raids can be foreseen without very great losses when the Squadrons F29, F123 and BM120 will be transformed into Sopwith Squadrons, which will raid in conjunction with the English Aviation.'

Until sufficient Sopwith $1^1/2$ Strutters could be made available, the French resorted to flying bombing raids at night while the British bombed by day. That strategy – which would be revived by the British and Americans in World War 2 – enjoyed more success, but not for long. Gen Sir Douglas Haig and Maj Gen Hugh Trenchard were opposed to long-distance bombing, since it diverted aircraft from the front, so 3 Wing was disbanded, reorganised, re-equipped with Sopwith Pup scouts and redesignated 3 Naval Squadron, RNAS.

Although a failure, the Oberndorf raid was a sprawling air battle by 1916 standards, and is all the more remarkable for the noteworthy airmen, for that time and for the future, who participated in it on both sides. Jean Pierre de Gaillard de la Valdène's claims were the second or third of an eventual five victories that were credited to him by the end of the war, the rest being scored as a fighter pilot in SPA95. Ray Collishaw would eventually account for 60 enemy aeroplanes destroyed by war's end, flying Pups with 3 Naval Squadron, Triplanes with 10 Naval Squadron and Camels as commander of 'Naval 3' and, after it was reorganised and redesignated on 1 April 1918, as No 203 Sqn, Royal Air Force.

On the German side, Ludwig Hanstein would go on to serve in *Jasta* 16 and command *Jasta* 35b until he was killed in action shortly after scoring his 16th victory on 21 March 1918. Kurt Haber's fifth victory was also his last, before transferring to *Jasta* 3 and being killed over Péronne on

A Voisin 8 (Canon) of VC113
commemorates the memory of
former member Adjutant Norman
Prince, who, after scoring his fourth
victory during the Oberndorf raid,
was mortally injured as he came in
to land (*US Air Force Museum*)

20 December 1916 by Sous-Lt Nungesser of N65. Ernst Udet's somewhat embarrassing victory was the second of an eventual 62, making him Germany's second-ranking ace. He went on to further fame as a stunt and test pilot at airshows and in motion pictures. He also rose to the rank of Generaloberst in Nazi Germany's Luftwaffe during World War 2, but the pressure and politics of his position ultimately drove him to suicide on 17 November 1941.

The day's star performer, Otto Kissenberth, added two SPADs and a balloon to his score while serving in *Jasta* 16. He then went on to command *Jasta* 23b, in which capacity he would meet the *Lafayette Escadrille* again.

As for the volunteers of N124, Oberndorf added more triumph and tragedy to their legend. Lufbery's victory had been his fifth, making him the first American ace in a war in which the United States had yet to be officially involved, and earning him another palm for his *Croix de Guerre*. Masson, miraculously unscathed, was awarded a *Croix de Guerre* with palm that acknowledged the outstanding circumstances under which he scored his first, and only, confirmed victory;

'Accomplished his mission to the finish, despite fuel exhaustion which befell him over German lines and forced him to return by volplaning.'

Norman Prince had scored his fourth victory, only to end his career and his life in a landing accident. He was driven ten miles to the hospital at Gerardmer, and seemed to be recovering until a blood clot developed in his brain, causing him to lapse into a coma. He died on 15 October at age 29, and like Rockwell was posthumously promoted to sous-lieutenant and made a *Chevalier de la Légion d'Honneur*.

Initially buried at a chapel near Luxeuil, Prince's remains were later reinterred in the *Memorial de l'Escadrille Lafayette* in the Parc Revue Villeneuve l'Étang, eight miles outside of Paris, but in the spring of 1937 his father had them moved again, to a vault in the National Cathedral in Washington, DC.

WITH *GROUPE DE COMBAT 13*

O n 18 October 1916, N124, its mission at Luxeuil completed, was ordered to Cachy. Again, there was a stop in Paris, where it picked up replacements Willis B Haviland, Fred Prince and Robert Soubiran on the 22nd.

Born in Minneapolis, Minnesota, on 10 March 1890, Willis Bradley Haviland had served in the US Navy from 1907 to 1911, studied electrical engineering at Iowa State College and served in the Illinois National Guard from 1912 to 1915 by the time he departed for France to serve in the American Field Service. On 26 January 1916 he joined the Foreign Legion in order to enter aviation, training at Pau and Buc with Prince, Soubiran and Robert Rockwell.

Soubiran, after being wounded in the knee by a shell splinter on 19 October 1915, had applied for a transfer into aviation, aided by the Rockwell brothers. After his release from hospital, he became a student pilot on 27 February 1916 and got his *brevet* in a Caudron on 27 May. Besides his mechanical expertise, Bob Soubiran brought along a Kodak camera with which he recorded an invaluable wealth of photographs documenting *escadrille* 124 for posterity.

N124 arrived at Cachy on 23 October 1916, and for the first time was permanently attached to a *Groupe de Combat* – GC13, led by Maj Philippe Féquant, at the disposition of *Général Commandant le Groupe des*

Sgt Frederick H Prince Jnr prepares to go up for a training flight in a Nieuport 11 equipped with Le Prieur rocket tubes. Norman's elder brother Fred arrived to take his place in N124 a week after Norman's death (*US Air Force Museum*)

Sgt Dudley Hill dons his flying gloves prior to climbing aboard the Nieuport 17 behind him, which bears the Seminole Indian head adopted by N124 as a unit insignia in late October 1916 (*Jon Guttman*)

Armées du Nord, which also included N65, N67 and N112. At that time, too, the first SPAD VIIs reached the squadron, although Nieuports would remain N124's principal fighters for several months to come.

According to Fred Prince, the mass flight to Cachy was marred by the loss of Sgt Laurence Rumsey, who later turned up at Delouze airfield. Over the past few months, Rumsey had become increasingly dependent on alcohol to bolster his nerves, and although he ignored his comrades' entreaties against flying, he was so inebriated that he became disoriented. Then, upon landing at the strange aerodrome he believed that he had come down in German territory and promptly set fire to his aeroplane!

Conditions at Cachy were appalling, dominated by rain, fog, mud, snow and leaky barracks. In *Flying for France*, McConnell remarked that until then the Americans thought they were waging 'a deluxe war', so their new accommodations – 'portable barracks newly erected in a sea of mud' – came as 'a rude awakening'. From mid-November to mid-January, there were only 12 days fit for flying, and there were seldom more than four planes and pilots fit to fly, although Pavelka was almost invariably among

Known as the 'Mother of the Legion' for her tireless work on behalf of American volunteers after the death of her son, Kenneth, at the front, Alice Standish Weeks opened her Paris apartment to Jim McConnell and numerous other N124 members, ultimately leading to the organisation of the Home Service for the American Soldiers Abroad. Her nephew, Henry Forster, also served as a fighter pilot in the *Lafayette* Flying Corps (*Henry Forster Collection via Jon Guttman*)

them. The resourceful Pavelka also installed ceilings in the *escadrille's* barracks, along with electrical connections that tapped into the camp's electric supply.

Another burst of creativity amid the squalor of Cachy occurred when Bill Thaw noticed the Seminole Indian head trademark on crates of ammunition from the Savage Arms Company and ordered one of the mechanics, Cpl Suchet, to apply it to the fuselage sides of N124's aircraft as a squadron insignia.

On 1 November Bert Hall left N124. Kiffin Rockwell had been his closest ally against Norman Prince's efforts to drive him out of the *escadrille*, and five days after Rockwell's death, Hall formally requested a transfer to N103. The orders arrived on 29 October and two days later, Emil Marshall, a former Legionnaire serving among N124's ground personnel, wrote in his diary that as Hall departed, he shook his fist at the other pilots and shouted, 'You'll hear from me yet'.

Whatever else can be believed from Hall's two contradictory books, *En l'Air!* and *One Man's War*, he was true to those parting words. On

26 November 1916 he sent a German aeroplane down just 200 metres from the French trenches, and he received another palm for his *Croix de Guerre* following this action He left N103 on 14 December, and subsequently accompanied French aviation missions to Russia and Rumania in January 1917. Hall was in France at the time of the Armistice, soon after which he married actress Della Byers. Post-war, he moved to Hollywood, where he produced and starred in two films, *A Romance in the Air* and *Border Patrol*, before Della divorced him in 1921.

Hall subsequently turned up in Hollywood or at bridge tournaments, as well as in China, where he concocted a scheme to sell obsolete Douglas bombers to warlord Gen Chang Hui-chang in 1929. Upon his return to California that summer, he was arrested for failure to carry out the contract, but Chang withdrew his suit after he received a portion of his cash advance, not wishing to lose face with a trial that would reveal how much he had been conned. Meanwhile, Hall went through another two wives before meeting vaudeville actress Elizabeth Chapline in January 1932. The two went to China the following month, and Hall resumed his arms trading, this time to Gen Ho Cho-kuo, until October 1933, when he was arrested in China and, on 1 November, pled guilty to a charge of 'engaging in illegal firearms importation into China for sale to military forces', and for receiving money under false pretences.

After serving two-and-a-half years in McNeil Island Federal Penitentiary in Washington, Hall returned to the lecture circuit, then went to work for Twentieth Century Fox studios as a technical advisor and script writer. He and Beth Chapline were married on 25 June 1937. His continuing money problems were somewhat alleviated when he wangled a $40,000 out-of-court settlement from Douglas for its failure to sell 20 aeroplanes to the Chinese during his spurious 1929 arms deal. He left Hollywood in 1939, and in 1944 he went into the toy business in Ohio.

In 6 December 1948, Hall's car went off the road, crashed through a fence and hit a utility pole outside of Fremont, Ohio. He had suffered a fatal heart attack. His wife's attempt to have his cremated remains buried at Arlington were refused due to his felony conviction, and Paul Rockwell subsequently turned down her request to have him interred at the Lafayette Memorial because he had not died in combat over France. Since Rockwell had made no such objection to Bill Thaw's interment in spite of his dying in the United States in 1930, it may be deduced that his real motive was to avoid having the roguish Hall there to tarnish the *escadrille's* idealised popular image.

On 20 January 1950, Hall's friend, test pilot Will D Parker, took off to scatter his ashes over his birthplace of Higginsville. Even then, Hall had the last laugh, as some of the ashes, caught in the propeller's slip steam, blew back into the co-pilot's eyes.

Hall was not the only N124 member to leave under exceptional circumstances. As they became more familiar with the grim realities of war, a number of the squadron's pilots had sought solace in alcohol, but Laurence Rumsey had come to depend upon it. On the same day Hall departed, Rumsey wrote of recently picking up a 110-hp Nieuport 17, but during a subsequent sortie he lost his five comrades in some heavy clouds, and upon emerging resumed formation with five aircraft, only to find that he had joined a German patrol – he escaped by hastily diving away. Later that month, he found Whiskey chewing on his new uniform cap and, as usual, only inclined to growl and tug harder when Rumsey commanded him to release it. Rumsey then struck the lion in the head with a walking stick, blinding him in his right eye. Feeling guilty and completely unnerved, Rumsey broke out in boils a few days later and had to be hospitalised. On 25 November he was dropped from N124's roll.

Returning to the United States, Rumsey earned a commission in the US Army's artillery corps in March 1918, but spent most of his post-war time playing polo, winning several awards. He did not 'cash in' on his service in N124, and did not attend any squadron reunions until his death in Buffalo, New York, on 11 May 1967.

While other members of N124 dealt with hardships on the ground, Lufbery pursued his standing vendetta, driving two enemy aeroplanes down too far behind their lines to be confirmed on 9 and 10 November 1916. They were the first of numerous 'probables' that he would claim, but the 10 November engagement over Haplincourt may in fact have resulted in the deaths of Ltn Max Hülse and Uffz Karl Münster of *Kampfstaffel* 30/KG 5, who came down ten kilometres south-southwest of Haplincourt. James Norman Hall reckoned that Lufbery's confirmed total of 16 was roughly half the number of aeroplanes he actually shot down, and Ed Hinkle claimed that if French confirmation standards had been less strict, 'Luf's' score would have been about 70.

German nocturnal raids on French airfields inspired Pavelka to convert his Nieuport into a nightfighter by devising instrument lights for his cockpit, powered by a wind-driven generator mounted on an interplane strut. After some test flights, he got the opportunity to apply his invention operationally on the night of 17 November, when German intruders dropped eight bombs on the aerodrome. Soon after taking off by the light

While a mechanic tends to the engine of Nieuport 17 N1844 at Cachy, on the Somme, in late October 1916, Lufbery smiles from the cockpit, Sgt Robert Soubiran looks on from the tail and Masson plays with Whiskey, N124's new lion cub mascot (*Greg VanWyngarden*)

The demoralising winter at Cachy drove Sgt Paul Pavelka to seek adventure in warmer climes by transferring to Salonika on 24 January 1917, serving in *escadrilles* N391 and N507. On 11 November that year he suffered injuries in a horse riding accident from which he died the next day (*Jack Eder Collection via Jon Guttman*)

of burning hangars, Pavelka's lights failed, perhaps due to a wire being jarred loose. With the airfield still under attack, he searched for the raiders, only to come under fire from French anti-aircraft gunners aiming at the sound of his engine. In spite of attempts to read his instruments using his cigarette lighter, Pavelka became lost and could only hope that his fuel would last until dawn.

The first glint of daybreak appeared on the eastern sky when his engine died, and Pavelka's luck held again as he glided over the barbed wire and came to rest in a patch of open ground. He then heard Cockney English accents through the morning fog, having landed at Martainville, 25 miles from Cachy.

In spite of the close calls he had survived, his failure to score any confirmed victories, the loss of good friends like Kiffin Rockwell and the gloom of late autumn took their toll on the normally cheery 'Skipper' Pavelka.

When the French asked for volunteers to serve in the *Armée de l'Orient* in Salonika, Pavelka decided that the change of venue might do him some good. He left N124 on 24 January 1917, and on 8 February he reported to N391 in Salonika. Although quarters were less than optimal, Pavelka wrote favourably of the food and the combat opportunities, and flew five hours a day. On 15 June he transferred to N507, and was subsequently awarded the *Croix de Guerre* with palm for fighting 'numerous air duels, following which he frequently returned with his machine riddled with bullets'. On 30 July, he reported that he had two aeroplanes, a Nieuport and an AR 1, with a Greek officer as his observer. He also wrote of the heat and that 'Malaria reigns supreme'. In mid-August, Pavelka and his driver were injured in an automobile crash, but he soon resumed flying with a wired jaw and bandaged knee.

On 11 November 1917, Pavelka visited a British cavalryman he had known while in the Foreign Legion. New horses arrived that same day, and after obtaining permission to ride one, Pavelka selected a mare that had not yet been broken, and was reputedly too vicious to ride. An accomplished horsemen from his days in the American West, Pavelka gave his British audience a good show until his ornery mount, sensing that she could not throw him, fell to the ground hard and rolled over her unwelcome rider. Pavelka was rushed to the hospital, but died of his injuries the next day. Buried at the Zietenlik Cemetery, his remains were exhumed in 1928 and reinterred in the *Lafayette Escadrille* memorial.

As if the stay at Cachy was not demoralising enough, N124 found itself regarded as a cause of national embarrassment when the US Secretary of State, yielding to German diplomatic protests, urged the French to cease referring to the squadron as *l'Escadrille Americaine*. On 16 November the French acquiesced, ordering the unit to use the more generic sobriquet of *l'Escadrille des Volontaires*. The Americans found that name too dull, but Dr Gros came up with a more emotive one. On 6 December N124 was officially renamed *l'Escadrille Lafayette*.

On 11 December Cpl Ronald Wood Hoskier joined the newly-renamed squadron. Born in South Orange, New Jersey, on 21 March 1896, Hoskier wrote prose and poetry, and edited the school paper at St George's School in Newport, Rhode Island, then enrolled at Harvard in the autumn of 1914. Meanwhile, his father, London-born financier and

Dudley Hill returns to Cachy from a mission in a Nieuport 17. After changing its nickname for diplomatic reasons from the *Escadrille Américaine* to the *Escadrille des Volontaires* – which the pilots judged too bland – N124 officially became the *Escadrille Lafayette* on 11 December 1916
(*Greg VanWyngarden*)

author Herman Charles Hoskier, and his mother, Harriet Amelia Hoskier, had gone to serve in Richard Norton's Ambulance Service in France. In February 1916, Ronald left Harvard to serve in the Norton-Harjes Ambulance Corps, then transferred to the Foreign Legion on 5 April, subsequently joining Edwin Parsons for flight training. Hoskier had spent some time between semesters studying flight at Hendon, in England, and he rose to the head of his training class before earning his *brevet* on 13 August 1916.

Lufbery ended 1916 and opened 1917 with fresh victories for the *Lafayette* log. On 27 December he downed an Aviatik southeast of Chaulnes, and on 24 January he drove down another between Chaulnes and Péronne, while de Laage logged a 'probable' in the same area. January also saw the arrival of more pilots – Cpl Edmund Genet on the 19th and Edwin Parsons on the 24th.

Thenault (second from left), Fred Prince and Masson visit the frontline trenches to confirm Lufbery's victory of 27 December 1916. Having closed out N124's 1916 victory log that day, 'Luf' opened it for 1917 by driving down an Aviatik on 24 January
(*Greg VanWyngarden*)

On 27 January 1917 N124 left Cachy for Ravenel, near St Just-en-Chaussée, in anticipation of a coming French spring offensive in the Oise and Aisne sectors. 'Ted' Parsons wrote of the squadron's new residence;

'The barracks weren't ready for us on our arrival, and for a week we lived underground like moles, sleeping on the dirt floors of the bomb shelters.'

The pilots froze in their cockpits and spent their time on the ground huddled under blankets. Parsons claimed that in his desperation for warmth, he slept with Whiskey, even though 'his fur smelled pretty high and he had a definite case of halitosis'.

Soon after the move to Ravenal, Thaw was leading a patrol between the Somme and Oise rivers when Parsons spotted five aircraft far below and waggled his wings excitedly. Thaw responded with an emphatic shake of his head, but Parsons disregarded it and dived on the specks, which quickly became identifiable as German two-seaters. They threw up a fusillade of lead and broke formation, allowing some to swing around onto the neophyte Nieuport pilot's tail.

Realising the trap he'd entered, Parsons banked and climbed at full throttle, expecting to die at any second. When he looked back, however, he saw another Nieuport scattering the Germans, driving one down out of control and another in flames. Parsons' word alone was not enough to confirm either victory for his benefactor, who he discovered upon landing to be Lufbery – the latter had just returned from leave minutes after Thaw's patrol had departed, so he had taken off to join him.

'Before I could blubber out my thanks', Parsons recounted, 'he proceeded to chew me out in that funny accent of his. "Don't you know you could have got in plenty trouble if I hadn't come?" He raked me over the coals for several minutes, and called me six kinds of a fool. I felt like a kid caught stealing jam. Then he said that I showed good spirit, and that we should have a drink.'

Parsons wrote that the episode taught him two lessons that were invaluable to any fighter pilot just entering combat. 'I was nowhere near the hotshot I had pictured myself to be', and 'none of us had any real idea of what we were getting into.'

On 8 February Stephen Sohier Bigelow, the 22-year-old son of a Boston investment banker, arrived. A Harvard graduate who was inspired by what he had read of Curtis' and Prince's efforts to form an all-American French unit, Bigelow had gone to Paris and joined the Foreign Legion on 16 April 1916. A crash during flight training had held up his *brevet* until

Cpl Stephen Sohier Bigelow peers down from the cockpit of a Nieuport 17 soon after joining the *Escadrllle Lafayette* on 8 February 1917 (*Jon Guttman*)

7 September – four days after Genet, costing Bigelow a wager that he would qualify first. His assignment to N124 was also delayed, and between 24 January and 8 February 1917 he flew missions with N102.

On 15 February Didier Masson left N124 with influenza, and upon recovery was assigned to Issoudun as an instructor. Fred Prince departed the same day, but not through any fault or desire of his own, however, but through the influence that his father – who did not want to risk losing his surviving son – had on the French government. A disappointed Prince served as an instructor for a time, as well as a liaison officer, ferry pilot and, briefly, a fighter pilot in SPA67. Joining the US Army, but unable to enter the air service, 1Lt Prince served in the Quartermaster Corps and finally as aide-de-camp to Brig Gen R E Bradley of the 16th Infantry Brigade, 8th Division. After a lifetime of conflict with his eccentric father, Fred Prince died of heart failure on 5 October 1962.

Flying conditions remained the exception in February 1917. During a morning patrol on the 2nd, Genet's oil froze and his engine burned up. Six days later he returned with his face badly frostbitten. In spite of that, he was up again on the 15th, attacking two Roland C IIs over Roye and forcing both to land behind their lines. 'It was so cold the aviators couldn't go up because the lubricating oil would freeze even with the motor going', wrote Emil Marshall on the 26th. 'Now, it is warmer, but still they don't fly', he added. 'The aviation field is ground that has been cultivated, and after thawing it has been rendered so soft that the machines can't land or leave the ground as the wheels stick in the mud'.

By 1 March three new pilots had joined N124's ranks. Born in Newton, Massachusetts, on 9 September 1884, Walter Lovell was a Harvard graduate who had served in the 1st Corps of Cadets, Massachusetts Volunteer Militia, before leaving his brokerage business to join the American Ambulance Service. He served with the latter organisation

Sgt Walter Lovell stands beside his Nieuport 17 (N1993), bearing a red inverted 'V' on the fuselage side. Lovell joined N124 on 1 March 1917 (*Greg VanWyngarden*)

Sgt Harold Buckley Willis poses with his Nieuport 17, displaying the Seminole emblem of N124. he joined the unit at the same time as his friend Lovell (*George H Williams Collection via Greg VanWyngarden*)

from February 1915 through to June 1916 alongside future N124 pilots James McConnell, Willis Haviland and Boston-born Harold Buckley Willis, a 1912 graduate of the Harvard Architectural College.

Recovering wounded men for the French 73rd Division, both Lovell and Willis were awarded the *Croix de Guerre* with star for courage under fire. Claiming to be fed up with his country's non-combatant rôle in a cause that he felt was right, Lovell enlisted in the Foreign Legion and then joined the air service in May 1916, followed by Willis in June.

With Lovell and Willis was the oldest *Lafayette* volunteer, Edward Foote Hinkle, who had been born the son of a shoe manufacturer in Cincinnnati, Ohio, on 22 May 1876. A graduate of Yale and Cambridge universities, Hinkle completed his studies in architecture and design at the École de Beaux Arts in Paris. Due to his mother's French ancestry, and his lifelong dislike of Germans, he joined the Foreign Legion on 20 July 1916. After learning to fly without damaging an aeroplane, he managed to get around the 28-year-old French age limit for aviation through the intervention of Dr Gros and fellow Yale man Bill Thaw.

Lufbery was made a *Chevalier de la Légion d'Honneur* the same day the new pilots arrived.

On 16 March Thaw and de Laage took Whiskey to Paris to see an oculist, and came back two days later with the mascot fitted with a glass eye, and a second lion. The pilots had decided that Whiskey needed companionship and, after eventually learning of a female lion cub for sale in Paris, chipped in to add her to the squadron's menagerie. The lioness got on so well with Whiskey that she was christened Soda, but she tended to spit and claw at any human who tried to pet her, with the significant exception of Lufbery.

Combat patrols resumed in earnest on 16 March, as British and French forces launched an offensive between Roye and Soissons. Three days later

Sgt Edward Hinkle and his SPAD VII. Joining N124 on 1 March 1917, he was the unit's oldest member, and designed its definitive insignia of a Sioux (Lakota) Indian head, which he thought more appropriately fierce than the earlier Seminole (*SHAA B76.706*)

Parsons, Genet and McConnell departed on patrol, but a clogged oil line caused Parsons' motor to seize up and he turned back. Flying on, Cpl Genet and McConnell encountered two German two-seaters near Ham and attacked them separately. The gunner of Genet's opponent shot away his main upper wing support and wounded him in the left cheek. Recovering, he closed until the two aeroplanes nearly collided, but failed to bring down his quarry. He then searched for McConnell for 15 minutes, until enemy anti-aircraft fire and the increasing likelihood of losing his upper wing convinced him to head home. To his horror, he learned that McConnell had not returned.

On 23 March GC13's Commandant Féquant reported that the crumpled remains of a Nieuport with the number 2055 on the rudder had been found in an apple orchard south of the village of Detroit Bleu. McConnell's body was found, stripped of his outer clothing, boots, identification and watch by German infantry. A peasant woman told the recovery party that she had seen McConnell engaging an enemy aeroplane when a second dived on him from behind and shot him down. He was credited to Ltn Heinrich Kämmerer of *Jasta* 20.

The death of the popular McConnell was a blow to all, but particularly devastating to Genet, who blamed himself for losing contact with him. More crushing news came on the 27th, when Genet received a letter from his mother, informing him that Gertrude Talmage, who he had loved since age 16, was engaged to another man, and had not had the heart to inform him. He wrote in his diary of avenging 'poor Mac', but added ominously that 'after this I vow I'll be more than reckless, come what may'.

N124 got three more arrivals on 30 March. Born in Oakland, California on 10 June 1885, Kenneth Archibald Marr was the son of naturalised Canadian immigrants who were living in Nome, Alaska, when war broke out. Enlisting in the American Ambulance Service, Marr had been gassed at Verdun, then joined the Foreign Legion and entered aviation 'to get a clean shirt and the blood off my clothes'.

Cpl Kenneth Archibald Marr with his Nieuport at Ravenal, shortly after his arrival on 30 March 1917 as a replacement for Jimmy McConnell, who had been killed in action 12 days earlier (*Greg VanWyngarden*)

Edwin Charles Parsons' Nieuport 17 came to grief reportedly while being flown by Kenneth Marr, who overshot the landing field (*Greg VanWyngarden*)

Lafayette members celebrate the news that the United States has entered the war on the Allied side as of 6 April 1917. They are, from left to right, William Dugan, Georges Thenault, Thomas Hewitt, Bill Thaw (with Fram and Soda), Raoul Lufbery, Alfred de Laage de Meux (walking off), Kenneth Marr (with unidentified squadron mascot), Edwin Parsons (with Whiskey) and Edward Hinkle (*SHAA B75.601*)

William Dugan had seen plenty of action alongside Paul Pavelka and Edmund Genet in Champagne and Verdun, but his attempts to get into aviation did not bear fruit until he was recovering from wounds in hospital in St Etienne in May 1916, when his father, and Dr Gros, helped him secure a transfer in early July. After training at Buc, Juvisy, Avord, Cazeaux and Pau, he finally arrived at N124 with Marr and 22-year-old Thomas Moses Hewitt Jnr, from Westchester, New York. The latter, after an unsuccessful attempt to join the RNAS, had gone through the now-familiar process of Richard Norton's Ambulance Service, the Foreign Legion and the *Service Aeronautique*.

Genet expressed misgivings about young 'Jerry' Hewitt's qualifications, and Thenault may be faulted for not breaking him in gradually. 'My first patrol was at the time of the St Quentin-Aisne retreat', Hewitt recalled. 'We were over a crack German battery. My only thought was keeping track of my comrades. I landed ten miles from my own field, and didn't know where I was'. That first experience seems to have undermined his confidence, and the next two months would do nothing to restore it.

The first week of April saw the Germans falling back to St Quentin and the Hindenburg Line, but for N124 the most momentous event was news that the United States had finally declared war on Germany on the 6th.

The next day, GC13 was ordered to advance 40 kilometres to Ham, which had been in German hands for nearly three years. N124 completed its move on the 8th, and Hinkle recalled that 'the Germans bombed the field five hours after we got there, burning five hangars'. At 1330 hrs that afternoon, however, de Laage downed a scout north of St Quentin, probably killing Ltn Roland Nauck of *Jasta* 6 in Albatros D III 234/16, and in the course of two more combats that day he scored his fourth confirmed victory, over a two-seater, north-northwest of Moy at 2350 hrs, killing Flgr Albert Glindkamp.

Lufbery downed a two-seater northwest of St Quentin on 13 April. Two days later, Andrew Courtney Campbell Jnr joined N124. Born in

Kenilworth, Illinois on 19 November 1891, 'Coty' Campbell was the son of a livestock broker. A playboy who sought thrills in fast cars, such as the Stutz Bearcat, and equally fast boats, he told his parents in mid-June 1916 that he was going to join the fighting in Europe, explaining, 'I am merely going to do in my small way for France what Lafayette and Rochambeau did for us'. Enlisting in aviation on 10 July, Campbell earned his *brevet* at Buc on 23 November. Upon his arrival at N124, he assumed a dual persona – on one hand a risk-taking jester in flight, and on the other a dependable wingman in combat. His fearlessness was to be tested the next day, when the *escadrille* lost another pilot.

Genet was ill when he awoke for the seven o'clock patrol with Lovell and Hewitt on 16 April, and the manoeuvring he did to evade a heavy dose of enemy flak north of St Quentin resulted in his complaining of a violently upset stomach when he returned at 0815 hrs. Nevertheless, he insisted on accompanying Lufbery at 1430 hrs, turning down Haviland's offer to take his place.

Flying low due to the clouds, the two came under more fire from *Kampf Flakzug* 47 over Moy, and Lufbery saw three shells explode about 100 yards aft of Genet's aeroplane. Genet turned back and 'Luf' followed him for four minutes to make sure he was all right, before resuming the patrol alone. Minutes after that, Genet's Nieuport 17 N1962 suddenly fell into a corkscrew dive with it's engine on full power, shedding a wing before crashing onto the road north of Montescourt, about 300 metres from where Jimmy McConnell had died. Buried under a casket draped with both the Tricolour and the Stars and Stripes, Edmond Genet was, at age 20, the first American to die since his country had officially entered the war. To a posthumous *Croix de Guerre* with two palms, he would later receive the *Médaille Militaire* in 1922.

In addition to its Nieuports, N124 had been receiving a gradual influx of SPAD VIIs, and also had Morane Saulnier P parasol two-seater MS 1112 on strength. Although most of the pilots distrusted the structural adequacy of the monoplane, Sgt Hoskier came to favour it, often flying the machine with De Laage's orderly, Cpl Dressy, as his gunner.

On 23 April the *Escadrille Lafayette* logged 18 combat missions, including the last one for the Morane before it was to be withdrawn from

Cpl Edmond Charles Clinton Genet in Paris on 4 September 1916 – one day after getting his *brevet militaire* at Buc, having graduated top of his class. He joined N124 at Cachy on 19 January 1917, but was killed in action on 16 April (*Lafayette Foundation*)

One of the first SPAD VIIs to arrive at Cachy in November 1916, S156 wears three red coup marks on the after fuselage and the butterfly emblem of Capitaine Thenault. Behind it is Soubiran's equally decorated Nieuport 17, N1977 (*SHAA B88.217*)

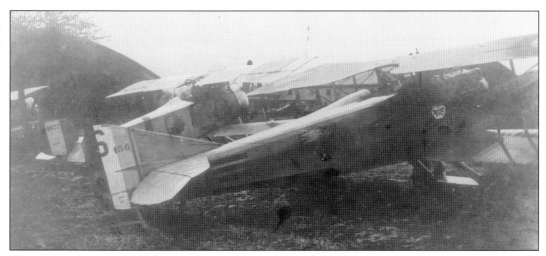

Convinced that two-seaters made better fighters than single-seaters, Sgt Ronald Hoskier preferred to fly missions in a Morane Saulnier P assigned to N124 (*Jon Guttman*)

A cross marks the spot where Hoskier and his gunner, Cpl Jean Dressy, died amid the wreckage of Morane Saulnier MS 1112 on 23 April 1917 after being shot down by three Albatros D IIIs of *Jasta* 20 (*Jon Guttman*)

the squadron. Hoskier, who had often claimed that a two-seater could do more damage in a dogfight than a single-seater, asked to pilot the Morane on its last sortie, hoping to prove his theory and 'really do some fighting'. Thenault reluctantly agreed, and Willis led a reconnaissance patrol over St Quentin, followed by Haviland and Thaw, with Hoskier and Dressy bringing up the rear in the Morane. As they entered a cloud, Hoskier became separated from the swifter scouts, and upon emerging from it he spotted an Albatros D III below him. Hoskier dived on it, only to be attacked in turn by three more fighters in a classic ambush.

Circling while Dressy manned the rear Lewis guns, Hoskier fought for 15 minutes, at one point attacking one of his adversaries head-on and on another sending one stricken Albatros spinning away. Finally, Dressy was down to 13 rounds and Hoskier had used up his ammunition when he was struck in the head and his aeroplane fell into a spin while flying at a height of 8000 ft. The wings folded and the Morane crashed just inside French lines. Its destruction was credited to Ltn Wilhelm Schunke of *Jasta* 20.

Upon learning of Hoskier's death, his squadronmates ran for his locker, knowing that his father had kept him well supplied with expensive Corona cigars. Two days later, his parents attended the service as he and Dressy were buried near Genet at Ham.

For his last action, Ronald Hoskier was posthumously awarded the *Croix de Guerre* with palm on 1 May. On that same day 21-year-old Ray Claflin Bridgman from Lake Forest, Illinois, arrived to take his place. With a Greek and Roman literature professor for a father and a writer for a mother, Bridgman studied history at Yale and was admitted to the *Phi Beta Kappa* honorary society in his junior year, only to leave in the spring of 1916 to work with the Red Cross. Although he hated war, while en route to Paris Bridgman decided to fight for France as an aviator.

Enlisting on 24 July, he got his *brevet* on 5 December and then trained on the Nieuport at Avord and practised gunnery and aerobatics at Cazeaux with his best friend, William Dugan.

April 1917 saw a steady influx of SPAD VIIs to replace N124's Nieuports. Here, *escadrille* members examine two newly-arrived examples at Ham aerodrome (*SHAA B96.136*)

Lufbery stands beside a SPAD VII at Cachy. He would use the new aeroplane to deadly effect in the year to come (*Lafayette Foundation via Jon Guttman*)

Vengeance for Genet and Hoskier was soon in coming, for on 24 April Lufbery downed an Aviatik east of Cerisy. Two days later Thaw, Haviland and Johnson spotted a formation of Albatros two-seaters and escort fighters. As they climbed to make a diving attack, they became dispersed among the clouds, so that Thaw and Haviland teamed up to shoot down one of the two-seaters near Juvincourt, while 'Chute' Johnson, finding another escort passing in front of him, fired at point-blank range and saw it emit black, oily smoke as it vanished in a cloud bank east of St Quentin. French ground observers, subsequently confirmed both victories – the second for Thaw and the first for Sgts Haviland and Johnson.

While the deaths of their comrades inspired most of the N124 pilots to seek revenge, they only reinforced Jerry Hewitt's timidity. He described one of the times he managed to cross the lines;

'Two Teuton craft, flying at about 2000 metres, were regulating artillery fire. My partner started down after them. The two machines

started down and headed for Laon. It did not take long to see that the chase was useless, so we started for home. The Teuton gunners put barrage after barrage in front of us. I lost my partner in the wild run for home, but upon landing found that he had reached there about ten minutes before me. I was awfully glad to get out of it.'

May saw new honours for Lufbery, as King George V ordered him to be awarded the Military Medal and the Aero Club de France struck a gold medal in his name, making him the first American to be so recognised.

On 12 May the unit got three new pilots. Charles Heave Dolan Jnr, the 22-year-old son of a Boston politician, first took an interest in aviation after watching Claude Grahame-White win a race around the Boston lighthouse in September 1910. He continued to study it while taking electrical engineering at the Lowell Technical Institute, and in 1914, Dolan left school and travelled to England, inspecting the first British-built aircraft magnetos and then working for Sperry Gyroscope Company Ltd in London.

While in Paris, he met members of N124, who saw his engineering skill as an asset and asked him to join them. When Sperry assigned him to work in Russia, Dolan resigned and joined the French Foreign Legion on 11 August 1916, then the air service. After earning his *brevet* in a Blériot on 11 March 1917, he was rushed into frontline service with N124 before he had received any gunnery training.

Cpl John Armstrong Drexel, the 25-year-old heir to a partner with the banker J P Morgan, hailed from Philadelphia and was a pre-war flyer who had set a world altitude record of 6604 ft in a Blériot on 10 August 1910. While at his father's Paris residence, Drexel enlisted in the French air service on 27 October 1916.

The third new arrival was Henry Sweet Jones, the 25-year-old son of Harford, Pennsylvania, politician Edward E Jones. He left Leigh University to join the American Ambulance Service in early 1916, serving for six months at Verdun and Fleury, before entering aviation via the Foreign Legion on 27 October. He earned his *brevet* on 16 March 1917.

Tragedy struck N124 anew late in the afternoon of 23 May. Lt de Laage was taking off in a new SPAD VII in his usual steep, climbing turn when

Bill Thaw's SPAD VII S1456 (left) shares the hangar with Bigelow's fully painted S331 and Masson's S1777, marked with red swastikas. Thaw scored his second victory, in concert with Sgt Willis Haviland, on 26 April 1917 (*Greg VanWyngarden*)

Sgt Henry Sweet Jones stands alongside red swastika-marked SPAD VII S1777, which was usually flown by Masson. 'Hank' Jones flew missions in it on 8, 9 and 10 September 1917 (*Greg VanWyngarden*)

the motor stalled at 200 ft, causing the aeroplane to side-slip and spin into the ground, killing him instantly. De Laage, who had wept at the funerals of every American who died in N124, was openly mourned in turn by the men of the unit. 'I was a witness to the accident, and was with him when he died', Bridgman wrote in a letter home. 'He was by far the noblest Frenchman I have known, and I believe almost the noblest man'.

Capitaine Thenault confers with Lt de Laage. The latter's death while test-flying a new SPAD on 23 May 1917 was a profound loss to the Americans. 'He was by far the noblest Frenchman I have known', wrote Raymond C Bridgman in a letter home, 'and I believe almost the noblest man' (*Paul A Rockwell Collection via Greg VanWyngarden*)

On 27 May a new executive officer arrived in the person of Lt Antoine Arnoux de Maison-Rouge, a former cavalry officer and fighter pilot with N67. There was no doubting Maison-Rouge's courage, but in contrast to the beloved de Laage, he kept himself aloof from the Americans, one of whom described him as a 'nervous, sensitive sort of Frenchman'. The highly strung Maison-Rouge, in turn, referred to the sometimes-cantankerous Americans as '*les sauvages.*'

On 3 June GC13 was ordered to a newly built aerodrome at Chaudun, behind Soissons in the *VIème Armée* sector. Parsons liked the new base, noting, 'The field was large and smooth, with plenty of landing space for all the six *escadrilles*'. There was, however, a deep irrigation ditch across the field, on which red markers were placed. Consequently, 74 members of GC13 avoided the ditch upon landing. The 75th, Hewitt, rolled right into it and flipped over, demolishing his SPAD but emerging unhurt. After cursing Hewitt in French and English, Thenault ordered him to bring in Soubiran's SPAD , since the latter was on leave in Paris. Hewitt did, only to run Soubiran's aeroplane into the ditch not ten feet from the site of his previous crash! Thenault grounded him.

At that point N124, now almost completely equipped with SPADs, was officially redesignated SPA124. At that time, too, the squadron insignia underwent a change. Hinkle, who had been promoted to sergeant after 30 combat hours, thought the original Seminole 'looked like an old woman with a drooping bonnet, and it wasn't very warlike. When I was a kid in Minneapolis, my uncle, a soldier, often told me stories about fighting the Sioux Indians. He had given me a head-dress taken in the wars'.

Inspired by that, he sketched a Lakota chief giving a war cry, which was approved by Thenault and the French authorities. Harold Willis designed an aluminium stencil and soon the *Lafayette* SPADs were sporting their definitive Indian heads, with reddish-brown faces and a white-feathered head-dress edged in blue to roughly replicate the French tricolour.

Characterising N124's transition of types and insignias is this photograph of SPAD VII S331, with the new Sioux Indian head in the process of being painted on the fuselage, along with 'eyes' on the cam covers, and a Nieuport 21 bearing the older Seminole marking. SPAD S331 was assigned to Cpl Stephen S Bigelow on 1 May 1917 (*B83.3461*)

On the morning of 12 June, Lufbery downed a two-seater over Sapignal for his tenth victory, but on the same day 'Pop' Hinkle left, having suffered a bout of pneumonia, followed directly by chronic bronchitis. Although well liked by his comrades, and victor over two 'unconfirmed' opponents in the three months he had served, Hinkle was unable to rejoin the squadron upon his release from hospital in September, and he spent the rest of the war serving as an instructor and ferry pilot. An architect and inventor after the war, Hinkle was made a *Chevalier de la Légion d'Honneur* on 14 July 1963, and died in Truth or Consequences, New Mexico, on 20 January 1967 at the ripe old age (for a World War 1 fighter pilot) of 90.

In contrast to such popular characters as Hinkle and Dolan, John Drexel did not get along well with his squadronmates, who made light of his Eton accent and eccentric ways. On 15 June his father arranged to have him withdrawn to serve as a liaison officer between the French and US armies. He had only served 36 days with the *escadrille*, and Parsons claimed that he never flew over the lines, so his subsequent promotion to major – the first SPA124 member to be commissioned in the US Army – was resented by those still in the squadron. An ardent Anglophile, Drexel died of a heart attack in Kent on 4 March 1958, and was buried in England.

James Norman Hall trains in a Caudron G 3 at Buc in April 1917. A veteran of British Army service – about which he wrote in his book, *Kitchener's Mob* – Hall joined SPA124 on 16 June 1917 and was seriously wounded in action ten days later (*Jon Guttman*)

The pilots of SPA124 pose together for a group portrait at Chaudun on 10 July 1917. They are, from left to right standing, Robert Soubiran, James R Doolittle, A Courtney Campbell, Edwin Parsons, Ray Bridgman, William Dugan, Douglas MacMonagle, Walter Lovell, Harold B Willis, Henry S Jones, David Peterson and Antoine Arnoux de Maison-Rouge. Seated, from left to right, are Dudley Hill, Didier Masson (holding Soda, with Fram in foreground), Bill Thaw, Georges Thenault, Raoul Lufbery and 'Chute' Johnson (holding Whiskey), Stephen Bigelow and Robert L Rockwell (*SHAA B76.813*)

On the same day Drexel left, Didier Masson rejoined SPA124, and 24 hours later James Norman Hall finally got his opportunity to join the *Escadrille Lafayette*. With him came two new volunteers. Douglas MacMonagle was born in San Francisco, California, on 19 February 1892, where his father died shortly after his birth. He attended universities in Switzerland and Germany, before taking up mining at the University of California at Berkeley in 1914, but he was expelled in the autumn of 1915 and went to France in October. There, MacMonagle volunteered for the ambulance service, earning the *Croix de Guerre* with star at Verdun, but being dismissed for 'drunkenness' on 20 September 1916. On 3 October MacMonagle joined the Foreign Legion and then the air service, obtaining his *brevet* at Buc on 13 April 1917 – the same day that 25-year-old David McKelvie Peterson, the son of a physician and coroner from Honesdale, Pennsylvania, earned his.

After graduating with a degree in chemistry at Lehigh University, Peterson had worked in a construction company in Pittsburgh and later at the Curtiss aviation plant in Buffalo, New York, where he learned to fly in his spare time. In September 1916 he went to France to join the air service, where he proved to be a natural pilot, with the added ability of being able to identify enemy aircraft before most of his comrades had even seen them. Those gifts, combined with an imperturbable coolness, resulted in his leading more patrols than any other *Lafayette* pilot by the time the squadron disbanded.

On 26 June a group of USAS officers on an inspection tour visited Chaudun, and Commandant Féquant ordered SPA124 to send up a patrol for them. Nine SPAD VIIs were slated to take-off, but one, S1386, suffered starting problems so that its pilot, Cpl Hall, took off several minutes late. Hall gamely strived to catch up, and spotted seven fighters five kilometres behind German lines. As he tried to join the formation, however, one of the fighters – which Hall now recognised as an Albatros –

turned and fired at him. Hall banked away, but a bullet went though his back, narrowly missing the left shoulder blade, and another grazed his face, cutting his goggles in two at the nosepiece. Hall spun down, and with his left side paralysed, held the stick between his knees and throttled down his engine before passing out.

The next thing he knew, he was lying on a stretcher in an Allied trench in Ostel Ravine, south of Courtecon. The wingless remains of his SPAD lay where it had pancaked on the sandbagged parapet of the forward trench. Hall was hospitalised at Neuilly and was subsequently awarded the *Médaille Militaire* and *Croix de Guerre*. On the other side of the lines, Vzfw Karl Schattauer of *Jasta* 23 was credited with shooting him down.

Hall's replacement was 23-year-old Cpl James Ralph Doolittle from Chicago, Illinois, the son of publisher James Reuben Doolittle. Having left Columbia University to join the Norten-Harjes Ambulance Service and then the *Service Aeronautique*, he arrived at Chaudun on 2 July 1917. While awaiting a combat assignment at Plessis-Belleville, Doolittle had wing-slipped into the ground on 2 May and suffered disfiguring wounds to the right side of his face – he spent eight weeks recuperating. Doolittle's short time in SPA124 would be equally unlucky.

Campbell, on the other hand, seemed to have so much luck that he was inclined to squander it. On 7 July he was test-flying Nieuport 23 N3578 over the field when he performed a power dive followed by a tight loop, only to hear his bracing wires snap and, as his aeroplane hung upside down, see the lower left wing break completely away. In spite of that, Campbell coolly counterbalanced his aeroplane as it came out of the loop and glided in for a perfect landing in a beet field ten kilometres away. When an ambulance arrived to retrieve his mortal remains, Campbell gleefully rode it back, stopping at several bars along the way to tell his story over drinks. The French awarded him the *Croix de Guerre* with star for saving the fighter, but Campbell treated the whole affair as a joke.

Sgt Andrew Courtney Campbell Jnr laughs at having cheated death in Nieuport 23 N3578 on 7 July 1917, having lost his left lower wing at an altitude of 1500 metres. He somehow managed to bring the Nieuport safely down in a beet field ten kilometres from Chaudun (*SHAA B96.121*)

Another view of Campbell and his Nieuport following his eventful test flight of 7 July 1917. The French awarded him the *Croix de Guerre* with star for saving the aeroplane, but Campbell regarded the whole affair as a joke (*Greg VanWyngarden*)

Replaced by SPADs as the *Escadrille Lafayette* was redesignated SPA124, one of the unit's Nieuport 24s arrives for new employment at the training field at Issoudun (*Jon Guttman*)

On 17 July GC13 moved to St Pol-sur-Mer in *Ière Armée* sector, on the Flanders front, where it was to support a new Allied offensive. The latter launched on the 31st, would become known as the Battle of Passchendaele. Several SPA124 pilots became lost during the flight, and Doolittle tried to land at an airfield to get his bearings, only to come under ground fire and see aircraft with black crosses taking off after him – the aerodrome was German!

Doolittle sought cover in the clouds, and when he emerged he saw a British Nieuport trying to prevent a German fighter's attack on a British balloon. As Doolittle tried to join in, he came under attack from two other German fighters, which struck him in the leg and the engine. Gliding toward British lines with his antagonists still in pursuit, he was wounded again by a British anti-aircraft shell before force-landing in a ploughed field. His Nieuport 24bis (N3616) turned over, reopening his facial wound. Doolittle was probably the 13th victory credited to Ltn Walter Göttsch of *Jasta* 8.

Although he was awarded the British Military Medal and the French *Croix de Guerre* with palm, Doolittle's wounds resulted in his being posted

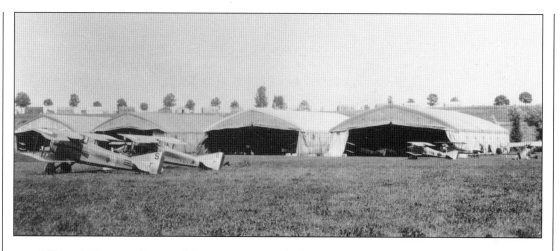

out of SPA124. He spent the rest of the war as a civilian flight instructor and test pilot at Dayton, Oho, but in the latter capacity he was injured again. After recovering, he went to Kenilworth flying field near Buffalo, New York, where he met and became engaged to May Louise Thomas. On 26 July 1918, as Doolittle took off in an experimental Curtiss aeroplane powered by the new Liberty engine, he lost control in a tight turn and crashed. His observer, Lawrence Dunham, died instantly and Doolittle passed away an hour later in hospital.

Other than the loss of the ill-fated Doolittle, Edwin Parsons recalled that 'the stay at Dunkirk provided a very pleasant interlude for the tough months to follow. It was a continuing round of sea bathing, poker and drinking parties with the pilots of several English squadrons near whom we were billeted'.

That would change dramatically on 11 August, when SPA124 moved to Senard, in *IIème Armée* sector. Parsons called it 'some really intensive air work – the most exhausting of all our campaigns'.

In contrast to the wayward weather experienced in Flanders, the area experienced 24 sunny days in a row, allowing constant flying. 'Three

SPAD VIIs and a remaining Nieuport 24bis of SPA124 occupy the aerodrome at Senard in August 1917 (*SHAA B88.1115*)

SPA124 SPAD VIIs line up outside the hangar at Senard in August 1917. With a new French offensive slated for the Verdun sector, the *Lafayette's* war was about to heat up again (*Steve St Martin Collection via Jon Guttman*)

shows a day', Parsons recalled, as well as 'nightly incursions of the German bombing squadrons'.

The French launched a new Verdun offensive on 17 August, and on the 18th 16 SPADs of SPA65 and SPA124 were assigned to escort 13 Sopwith 1 1/2 Strutters of GB1 on a daylight raid against the railroad yard at Dun-sur-Meuse and the ammunition depot at Banthéville. 'They split us into two groups, one on each side of the bombers', Willis recalled. 'Instead of giving us freedom for manoeuvring, as they should have, they told us to stay with the slower, bigger aeroplanes'.

Consequently, the escort fighters had to zigzag to maintain their positions, and the formation soon came under attack by German fighters. In spite of the escorts' efforts to prevent it, the enemy claimed two bombers, although only one was confirmed – Sous-Lt André Aignan and Cpl Paul Boudon of Sop111 were forced to land at Malancourt, where they became PoWs.

Sgt Walter Lovell scored his only confirmed victory, and earned the *Croix de Guerre* with palm, when he and Maréchal-des-Logis Marcel Paris of SPA65 teamed up to bring down an Albatros in flames near Cierges, although the Germans recorded no fatalities in the day's action. Sgt Bigelow's patrol came under attack from a number of German fighters, but he succeeded in driving them off. An Albatros got on the tail of the other flight leader, Sgt Parsons, but Willis drove it down in a dive.

Willis then found himself attacked by two other Germans, and in spite of making an Immelmann turn he was unable to lose one of them, who hit and disabled his engine. 'He followed me all the way, down, this fellow and some of his friends', Willis said. 'He very properly tried to shoot me down, because he didn't know whether or not I'd get my engine going

Sgt Walter Lovell and his mechanic, Gement, pose before take-off. The pilot assigned to the SPAD with the red star personal marking parked behind them remains unknown (*George H Williams Collection via Greg VanWyngarden*)

Sgt Harold B Willis' SPAD VII S1615 in German hands after he was brought down by Ltn Wilhelm Schulz of *Jasta* 16 at Dun-sur-Meuse on 18 August 1917. Willis' green initial can be plainly seen on the left upper wing (*Greg VanWyngarden*)

again and get back to the lines'. Although hit in his windscreen and his goggles shot away, Willis managed to land on a hillside near Dun-sur-Meuse. His victor landed nearby, and protected Willis from possible abuse by German infantry. They then went to have breakfast at the German's unit – *Jasta* 16 – before Willis was taken to the fortress at Montmédy that afternoon.

There were two claimants to having shot down Willis – Uffz Max Holtzem, who was a former Pfalz test pilot recently assigned to *Jasta* 16, and Ltn Wilhelm Schulz, who ultimately got the credit on the basis of his rank. Holtzem, who spent the last decades of his life in the United States, always prided himself on an old-fashioned sense of chivalry and an aversion to killing, so Willis' description of his last antagonist shooting at him suggests that it was more likely Schulz.

Jasta 16's mechanics restored Willis' SPAD VII (S1615) to some form of airworthiness, but they had to replace a wheel with one from an Albatros D V. That proved to be a mistake, as Holtzem found out when he tried to test-fly it and found the aeroplane taxiing in a circle because of the larger-diameter German wheel. The motor, running on just one magneto, had also lost some 100 hp, but Holtzem managed to wring just enough power out of it to clear a hangar, then lost it and came down in a nearby marsh that his squadron used for target practice. Carried back to terra firma on a groundcrewman's shoulders, Holtzem remarked, 'I think I am right in saying that everyone felt relief now that the SPAD had come to its end'.

As a PoW, Willis spent time at Karlsrühe, Landshut, Gutersloh, Holstein, Bad Stuer and Villingen. The latter prison, to which he was sent on 1 July1918, was the worst – and the first where he came into contact with fellow Americans, including US Navy Lt Edouard Izac, who had been captured by the submarine *U-90* after it had sunk his vessel, the transport *President Lincoln*, on 21 May 1918. On 5 October the

Americans made a mass breakout attempt, during which Willis and Izac managed to escape and together made it across the Rhine to Switzerland, and from there were able to get to France on the 17th.

Willis, who had been commissioned a sous-lieutenant by the French and a major by the USAS, received the *Médaille Militaire* for his escape, while Izac was awarded the Medal of Honor. Willis again served in the American Field Service during World War 2, until France fell in 1940. Later, as a US Army Air Forces colonel on Gen Carl A Spaatz's staff, he helped create another *Escadrille Lafayette*, this time with Free French pilots. Harold Willis pursued architecture after the war, until his death from cancer on 17 April 1962.

On 20 August Bigelow, in SPAD VII S387, was leading an escort flight when he encountered eight enemy fighters and engaged six that were diving on a Sopwith bomber. Driving them down, he engaged another German in a head-on gun duel, but was struck twice in the face by bullet fragments. Loath to leave his unit in the midst of intense aerial activity, Bigelow ignored Thenault's order to seek immediate medical treatment, but by the second week of September his wounds became so infected that he was sent to hospital. He was discharged from French service as physically unfit for active service in January 1918. Unable to deal with the anticlimax of post-war civilian life, Bigelow's spirits deteriorated, as did his health, from tuberculosis and alcohol, until his death in Boston on 6 January 1939, aged 44.

On 4 September Sgt Parsons scored his first victory, over a Rumpler C IV, near Cheppy, his victims probably being Uffz Otto Meyer and Ltn Otto Stumpp of F. Fl. Abt. (A) 278. Lufbery downed a second enemy aeroplane east of Cheppy five minutes later.

On 19 September Sgts Peterson and Marr spotted six Albatros scouts attacking a three-seater reconnaissance aeroplane of F44, flown by Sgts Desthuilleirs and Dauguet and Maréchal-des-Logis Viallet. They rushed

Willis' SPAD was restored to flyable condition, complete with German crosses and a replacement Albatros D V wheel on the right axle stub that proved to be its undoing when Uffz Max Holtzem tried to test fly it (*N H Hauprich album*)

Sgt David McKelvie Peterson beside a SPAD VII that wears Thenault's butterfly emblem on its cowling. Peterson scored his first victory – and his only one with SPA124 – on 19 September 1917 (*Jack Eder Collection*)

to its assistance, and in the course of the fight an Albatros went down. Peterson, determined to see it crash, pursued the cripple to the ground, unmindful of the enemy ground fire that peppered his SPAD at low altitude. The victory was credited to all five Allied participants, and Peterson was awarded the *Croix de Guerre* with palm for the extraordinary aggressiveness he displayed.

That same day Courtney Campbell struck again – literally. As de Maison-Rouge was leading a patrol back to Senard, Campbell began playfully bouncing his wheels on his risible executive officer's upper wing, until he miscalculated and his wheels broke through the fabric, locking the two SPADs together. Miraculously, Campbell was able to break free again and both pilots landed safely, but de Maison-Rouge's nerves gave out amid an explosion of rancour toward all the '*sauvages*' Americans.

A SPAD VII of SPA124 takes off. Unfortunately, the pilot of this band and star-marked machine remains unidentified (*SHAA B84.2130*)

Thenault sent him to the rear for an extended rest, and he was officially dropped from SPA124's rolls on 6 October. Lt de Maison-Rouge returned to combat with SPA78 on 14 January 1918, serving gallantly with that unit until he was killed in action on 31 May.

On the same day that Peterson was opening his account and Campbell was unhinging de Maison-Rouge, Jimmy Hall, recovered from his wound, returned to the front, but due to a bureaucratic error, it was not to SPA124, but SPA112. While with that unit, the fuel pump of his SPAD VII failed, and as he tried to glide in for a landing, he struck a wire fence and crashed, breaking his nose against the instrument panel.

On 22 September Marr, Jones and MacMonagle were jumped by four Albatros D Vs, two of which singled out Marr, who nevertheless drove one off before the other shot through his elevator cables. At that point Jones chased off Marr's assailant, who may have been Ltn Emil Thuy of *Jasta* 21, who claimed a SPAD over Hill 304 for his 14th victory.

By alternately revving his engine up and down, however, Marr managed to control his plane in a 6000-metre descent into the Forêt de Hesse. When French soldiers came along, Marr commandeered their car, drove to fetch mechanics and spare cable, made the necessary repairs and flew his

Adjutants Pierre de Cazenove de Pradines and Henri Perroneau of SPA81 discuss their latest combat with Lt Thaw amid the wreckage of their victim on 22 September 1917 (*Pierre de Caznove de Pradines album via Jon Guttman*)

aeroplane back to Senard. After refilling the tanks, he was ready to fly another mission that same day.

Elsewhere, at 1342 hrs on the 22nd Lufbery downed a two-seater over Bois de Cheppy. Soon afterward, he became the first American since Bill Thaw to receive a commission while in SPA124, as a sous-lieutenant. By that time, too, he had become so famous that babies were being named for him and culinary dishes were being created in his honour, such as Aubergines (eggplant), Faison (peasant), Poisson (fish) and Parfait Lufbery. Hispano Suiza presented him with one of its sport cars. Women threw themselves at him, both as lovers and (vainly) as prospective wives.

That afternoon, MacMonagle and Dolan got a 48-hour pass to visit Paris. It was MacMonagle's first leave since he had joined the American Ambulance Service in 1915, and he spent some of it at the apartment of his mother, who was a volunteer nurse at a Red Cross hospital. He was well-behaved in her presence in the mornings, but drank heavily afterward, compelling Dolan, who was a teetotaller, to steer him to bed at the hotel one night, and to the train station the next.

When they returned early on the morning of the 24th MacMonagle, tipsy on champagne, woke up Capitaine Thenault to announce his return. Thenault, outraged, ordered the American into his flying togs for the first morning patrol. Dolan, who realised his comrade was in no shape for such a mission, offered to take his place, but MacMonagle, once committed, rejected his offer. After pouring coffee into MacMonagle and asking

Sgt Charles Heave Dolan Jnr poses in his pyjamas with as little concern as he would show in combat. A lifelong teetotaller, Dolan served as 'designated driver' decades before the concept became fashionable – sometimes bringing drunken squadronmates back in the bed of the unit truck (*SHAA B86.695*)

Sgt Dolan stands beside one of his monogrammed SPAD VIIs (possibly S3148), which he flew in the *Escadrille Lafayette's* last days, and continued to fly with the 103rd Aero Squadron until May 1918 (*Jon Guttman*)

Dolan in his SPAD VII, which bore a red and white monogram of his initials CHD. A steady, reliable wingman, Dolan did not score a confirmed victory until October 1918, while serving in N124's USAS successor, the 103rd Aero Squadron (*Jon Guttman*)

Lufbery to keep an eye on him, Dolan retired, while 'Luf' led 'Doc' Rockwell and MacMonagle into the air – Parsons was left behind, for his SPAD would not start.

As the trio reached 15,000 ft, Rockwell noticed MacMonagle flying erratically, while Lufbery spotted eight Albatros D Vs patrolling 1500 ft above them. 'Luf' gestured for his men to follow him above and behind the Germans, but as he began his steep climb, MacMonagle turned to engage an Albatros that was descending out of the sun. Before Rockwell could head him off, he was amid the enemy patrol, two of whose members got on his tail. Moments later MacMonagle's SPAD VII (S2119) spun down to crash near Thiaucourt.

Soon afterward Parsons, who had finally got his balky engine running, caught up with the surviving *Lafayette* men and helped them drive the Germans off. It became Carl Dolan's sad duty to recover MacMonagle's body that morning, and to inform his mother of his death when she came to visit the *escadrille* later that day.

The only SPAD claim made in the Verdun sector on 24 September was by Ltn Otto Kissenberth, the Bavarian hero of the Oberndorf raid, who was now commanding *Jasta* 23 – he claimed a SPAD between Vauquois and Avocourt. It was his 17th kill, and he would bring his total to 20 before being injured in the crash of a captured Camel on 29 May 1918. While convalescing, Kissenberth was awarded the *Orden Pour le Mérite* and finished the war as CO of the Schliessheim flying school, but he was killed while mountaineering in the Bavarian Alps on 2 August 1919.

Jimmy Hall, who regarded 'Mac' as one of his best friends at SPA124, was still recuperating from his crack-up at SPA112 when he learned of

Ltn Otto Kissenberth, who had first encountered N124 over Oberndorf on 12 October 1916, was commanding *Jasta* 23 when he was credited with shooting down MacMonagle almost a year later. He would finish the war with 19 victories, and the *Orden Pour le Mérite* (*Greg VanWyngarden*)

MacMonagle's death. On 3 October, Hall succeeded in obtaining a transfer back to the *Escadrille Lafayette*.

Hard times were not yet over for SPA124, for on 25 and 27 September the Germans bombed Senard, setting a hangar on fire. On the 29th GC13 moved to Chaudun for the Malmaison offensive. Thenault fell ill at that time, and for the next month Lt Thaw took command of the squadron.

One pilot who did not accompany the *escadrille* to Chaudun was Willis Haviland, who transferred to SPA102, in which he served from 1 October through to 28 December. He then joined the US Naval Reserve in Paris as a lieutenant (senior grade). In that capacity, Haviland was chief pilot at the US Naval Air Station at Dunkirk, flying antisubmarine patrols until 23 March 1918, when he joined 13 Naval Squadron, RNAS. From there, he went to Italy on 2 May 1918, and after training in Macchi flying boats, he took command of naval air station at Porto Corsini.

On the first day of October, 'Court' Campbell's luck finally ran out. Dolan was leading him and Jones on patrol when they encountered four Hannover CL IIIs north of Soissons. As they dived to attack, the Germans

formed a circle for mutual protection, and soon after the engagement began Dolan dropped out with engine trouble. Jones tried to attack a Hannover from below, only to see a panel slide open and a machine gun open fire on him. Jones volplaned back to Chaudun with 34 holes in his fuselage and wing. Campbell's SPAD VII (S4245) never returned, and it was not until November that the Germans dropped a map showing where he had been killed, and a message of his having been buried near Pargny.

Campbell was credited to Uffz Kurt Andres and Vztr Karl Waldemar Ritscherle of *Schutzstaffel 8*. In his own account of the action Ritscherle, then 19, remarked that Andres was not his usual pilot, and that they were on a familiarisation flight;

'It happened that, in the course of what could be called a real air fight with an American who was flying behind us under French colours in a SPAD fighter plane, my replacement pilot got so excited that, instead of stepping on the rudder bar, he activated the elevator and really pumped it. Understandably, that had the effect of our flying along in wavy lines. The SPAD, which flew behind us at a slight distance, sometimes below us, sometimes above our tail, fired whenever he could. All I could do was return the fire. Now, to make a long story short, I shot my own tail assembly to pieces, but the Yankee breathed his last – I clearly saw the grey cloud of smoke with which he went spinning down.

'When I returned to Liesse there was great joy, but well-wishers did not have to reach out to touch us, for we slid across the field like a fish, as the undercarriage was literally shot off and hung on by only two struts.'

After scoring three victories as a gunner, Karl Ritscherle was commissioned a Leutnant der Reserve on 27 December 1917, trained as a fighter pilot and, on 22 June 1918, he returned to the front with *Jasta* 60, with which unit he was credited with another five victories. He returned to active service in the Luftwaffe during World War 2, and was reported killed in action over England on 24 August 1940.

On 6 October 1917 SPA124 got a new French executive officer. Louis Verdier-Fauvety had started the war with the *8ème Hussards* on

Campbell with his Nieuport 24bis N3772 at Chaudun. He was flying a SPAD when his luck ran out on 1 October 1917 (*H Hugh Wynne Collection via Jon Guttman*)

Lt Louis Verdier-Fauvety (left) with Capitaine Lamy, commander of SPA65, an unidentified *poilu* and Lt Louis Sejourné of SPA65. A friend of Charles Nungesser's, Verdier replaced de Maison-Rouge as SPA124's executive officer, and swiftly made a good impression on the Americans (*SHAA B83.1283*)

10 October 1914, but was severely wounded soon after. Upon recovery, he had enlisted in the air service on 26 February 1916, and joined N65 on 18 November. In addition to becoming one of Charles Nungesser's best friends, Lt Verdier had come to admire and befriend the Americans at neighbouring N124, so when Thenault duly asked him to replace de Maison-Rouge, he enthusiastically accepted. Verdier proved to be an able and unflappably courageous flight leader, and his cheery nature had a swift effect on the battered morale of the American pilots, who paid him the ultimate compliment by referring to him as the second de Laage de Meux.

Didier Masson, suffering from cold and fatigue, left SPA124 for the last time on 8 October, serving in the defence of Paris with N471 from 10 to 28 October, and as an instructor at Issoudun until 1 November 1918. His postwar career included exporting chewing gum, serving as field manager for Pan American Airways in Belize and as French consul to British Honduras, resigning from the latter after France surrendered to the Germans in June 1940. He then resided in Mexico, until his death on 2 June 1950.

The Malmaison Offensive officially got under way on 10 October 1917, and on that same day Lufbery claimed six enemy aircraft destroyed, though none could be confirmed. He had better luck on the 16th, downing a two-seater in flames between Vauxillon and Hurtebisel.

The *Escadrille Lafayette* suffered another melancholy loss in October, after Whiskey knocked yet another visiting officer to the ground, then chewed up his bright tunic and visor cap. The playful lion had chosen the wrong victim this time – it was GC13's commander, Commandant Féquant, who after being narrowly dissuaded from ordering both lions shot, had them removed to the Jardin des Plantes. On 17 October, Lufbery and Hinkle took SPA124's most famous mascots for their last

French mechanics play with Soda beside Hinkle's SPAD and a yawning Whiskey. Acquired as a companion for Whiskey, Soda got on well with him and Fram, but became surly among most human company (*George H Williams Collection via Greg VanWyngarden*)

Lufbery plays with Soda and Whiskey at Chaudun in October 1917. 'Luf' was one of the few humans who was able to get along with the temperamental Soda (*SHAA B87.3893*)

ride in a *camion*, which Whiskey enjoyed immensely – until he heard the cage door clang shut. 'We visited Whiskey whenever we had Paris leave, and he always recognised us', Hinkle said, but added ruefully, 'Both Whiskey and Soda died soon after the war of rheumatism, or maybe loneliness'.

Lufbery had another of his busy days on the 24th, starting with a two-hour dawn patrol in which he engaged and shot down two German fighters. After replenishing his fuel and ammunition, 'Luf' encountered three more German fighters, and sent two of them crashing into the ground. During his third sortie of the day, he claimed two more victories. In most of his combats, however, the only witness was his wingman, Ed Hinkle, and the French required two more to confirm a victory. Consequently, only one of the two-seaters, which Lufbery had downed over Courtecon in concert with Lt Paul Louis Malavialle of N69, was confirmed as his 14th and Malavialle's ace-making fifth victory.

Adjutant Lufbery poses beside a SPAD VII. On 24 October 1917 he claimed six victories in three combats, but only one was confirmed (*SHAA B88.1158*)

Ironically, the only German fatality for the day in that area was single-seat fighter pilot, Ltn Heinrich Breidt of *Jasta* 13, who was killed at Chevregny, five kilometres west of Courtecon. It would seem, then, that Lufbery's official victims survived, while one of those *not* credited to him may, in fact, have died at his hands.

The 24th also saw the departure of Adjutant Lovell, who had established a solid record as one of SPA124's most dependable flight leaders, to take a captain's commission with General Headquarters to the American Expeditionary Force after his medical tests indicated a hearing loss and colour blindness, which effectively kept him behind a desk for the balance of the war.

Promoted to major in August 1918, Walter Lovell later served as a chief aviation instructor in the United States until he resigned in January 1919. He then became involved in a number of businesses until his death on

9 September 1937, after a three-month illness from a brain abscess, at Bayshore, Long Island, New York.

On 8 November the 38th, and last, American pilot to serve in SPA124 arrived. Born on 2 October 1892, Christopher William Ford was the son of immigrants – an Irish father and a German mother – but was orphaned at an early age. Raised by an aunt on New York's lower east side, he sold newspapers while educating himself through George Washington University.

Ford was a reporter with the *Wall Street Journal* in 1914, and took flying lessons at the Marjorie Stinson Flying School at San Antonio, Texas, in 1916. In March 1917 he joined the American Red Cross, but after arriving in France he learned that the United States had entered the war and he joined the French air service through the Foreign Legion on 26 April 1917.

Chris Ford's humble origins initially handicapped his acceptance in a squadron of predominantly educated men from established families, but he tackled that the same way as he had in his youth. He volunteered for extra combat missions, and his dedication soon turned him into one of the *escadrille's* most popular members. As he became more experienced and confident, he began to paint red, white and blue lightning bolts on the fuselage and wings of his SPAD VII.

Lufbery teamed up with Sgts Vidal and Rousseau, Brigadier Wurtz and Cpl Cabot of SPA88 to down a two-seater in flames south of Ployart on 2 December, their victims in this case probably being Ltn Erich Pohl and Otto Heilmann of Royal Saxon F. Fl. Abt.(A) 255. In a later solo effort that same day, 'Luf' drove another two-seater down emitting black smoke over Laval, which was confirmed as his 16th victory.

Skilful though he was, Lufbery suffered from rheumatism for much of his flying career, which required him to go on periodic leaves and caused him constant pain when he flew. He persisted, however, and a letter he wrote to aviation writer Jacques Mortane on the occasion of his 2 December double victory revealed his principal motivation;

SPA124 mechanics with S1777.
Sous-Lt Lufbery flew the swastika-
bedecked aeroplane when scoring
his final victories in October and
December 1917
(*Greg VanWyngarden*)

The *Escadrille Lafayette's* first
confirmed victory of 1918 – and its
last before its dissolution on 18
February 1918 – was scored by Sgt
James Norman Hall, shown at
Soissons on 26 October 1917. On
1 January 1918 Hall downed an
Albatros D Va near Brimont,
probably killing Uffz Albert
Meinhardt of Royal Saxon *Jasta* 21
(*Jon Guttman*)

'Just think. It was three years to the day that Marc Pourpe fell on the field of honour. Each anniversary I have made an effort to avenge him. I want to dedicate the victims to him. Our great friend should be satisfied with the manner in which I honour his memory, although never on God's green earth will he receive all the honour he deserves.'

The following day, SPA124 was ordered to La Cheppe and La Noblette, north of Châlons in the *IVème Armée* sector, and its American personnel advised to obtain releases from the *Service Aeronautique* in order to obtain USAS commissions. All would do so except Parsons, who had gone on leave in November 1917, during which he spoke with former squadron mates who told him of unsatisfactory conditions in the USAS, and of long delays in returning to combat with that organisation. By the time he returned in January 1918, Parsons had decided to remain with the French.

While their paperwork was being processed, the rest of SPA124's pilots were officially released from duty, although they would continue flying for the next two months as 'civilians'. During one of those 'civilian' patrols on the first day of 1918, James Norman Hall scored his first and the *Escadrille Lafayette's* 37th, and last, official victory.

Hall claimed that during a patrol with Thaw, his 'keen sense of the glory of flying, and the wonder of it' caused him to lose track of his leader. A short while later he saw an aeroplane about half-a-mile away, and thinking it to be Thaw, climbed above it to give his leader a playful surprise. As Hall dived to within 100 yards, however, he identified the aeroplane as a German fighter and opened fire until he saw it disappear into a cloud, apparently out of control. When he returned to La Noblette, he found that Thaw had landed 20 minutes earlier. Hall subsequently learned that French infantry had seen the enemy fighter crash between the lines near Fort Brimont. 'Furthermore', he wrote in a letter to a friend, 'one wing of the German machine fell in the French lines, and confirmation came in before I myself had landed, after the fight'.

Hall regarded it as revenge for Douglas MacMonagle's death, and the death that day of Uffz Albert Meinhardt of Royal Saxon *Jasta* 21 at Betheny, southeast of Brimont, suggests that such would indeed have been the case. In a separate letter, written on 9 March, Hall mentioned the ironic probability that that success was responsible for his entering the USAS as a captain, rather than a lieutenant.

SPLIT METAMORPHOSIS

On 16 January 1918, Capitaine Thenault left SPA124, again leaving Thaw in command. On 18 February the pilots' USAS commissions arrived and SPA124 was officially redesignated the 103rd Aero Squadron. It was only fitting that the squadron's commander, now Maj Thaw, had been one of N124's founding fathers, and had scored two victories while serving in it. SPA124, meanwhile, was reformed as a French unit, under the command of Lt André d'Humières.

Both SPA124 and the 103rd Aero Squadron operated together from La Noblette aerodrome during the spring of 1918, as components of GC21, commanded by Capitaine Lucien Couret de Villeneuve. Also in the group were *escadrilles* SPA98, SPA157 and SPA163, to be joined later in the year by SPA164.

As with the famed GC12, whose SPADs were identified by the common theme of storks in various attitudes of flight, all of GC21's French squadrons used diagonal fuselage bands of different colour combinations for identification – yellow-black-yellow for SPA98, white for SPA124, blue for SPA157, red-black-red for SPA163 and blue and red for SPA164. In contrast to its French sister units, however, the 103rd Aero Squadron

SPA124's SPADs undergo a marking change at La Noblette soon after the unit had been redesignated the 103rd Aero Squadron (*Livinston Irving via Jon Guttman*)

'inherited' the Sioux Indian head that its aircraft had worn in its *Escadrille Lafayette* days, and retained the use of personal motifs, rather than numbers, for individual identification.

The 103rd Aero Squadron's first victories in USAS service were scored by a 1Lt Paul Frank Baer, an Ohio-born volunteer who never made it into SPA124, but who was assigned to SPA80 through the *Lafayette* Flying Corps (LFC) – an expanded organisation that farmed out the almost 200 American volunteers to other French units. On 11 March 1918, Baer opened the 103rd's account with an Albatros over Cenay-les-Reims, and five days later he and Sous-Lt Levrier of SPA38 downed an Albatros two-seater over Nogent-l'Abesse.

The squadron's third victory, over a German scout near Somme-Py on 27 March, involved a team-up by three old SPA124 members – Maj Thaw, Captain Hall and 1Lt Ford – against three two-seaters and five fighters. Ford's gun jammed early in the action, but he remained above his comrades, diving on any German who got on their tails for almost 20 minutes. All three pilots were credited with one of the enemy scouts, and Hall downed a second over St Étienne-à-Arnes to raise his tally to three.

The 103rd lost three of its *Lafayette* members on 31 March, when Jimmy Hall, Ken Marr and Dave Peterson were reassigned to the 94th Aero Squadron. On 10 April GC21 moved up to Bonne Maison, near Fismes, to join the French ground forces opposing the last great German offensive of the war. Two days later, Baer downed an Albatros over Proyart.

On 20 April Bill Thaw and 1Lt George Evans Turnure (an LFC pilot who had served in SPA103) burned a kite balloon at Montaigu, and 15 minutes later Thaw sent an enemy scout down in flames over Reservoir-Merval, bringing his total to five. Baer scored his fifth victory three days

Capt James N Hall stands alongside a SPAD XIII of the 103rd. Hall scored his second and third victories with the unit (*George H Williams Collection via Greg VanWyngarden*)

A panel of fabric from SPAD VII S5301, flown by Maj William Thaw and 1Lts George Turnure, Hobart A H Baker and Drummond Cannon in the 103rd Aero Squadron. While commanding the 103rd, Thaw shared in three more victories, achieving acedom
(*Alan D Toelle via Jon Guttman*)

later, having achieved acedom in a month-and-a-half, whereas it had taken almost two years for Thaw to do so. Thaw's achievements, however, had come in spite of his having 20/80 vision, a hearing defect and a debilitating knee injury. Under ordinary circumstances, he would not have been allowed in the military at all, but by the time Thaw left the USAS, he was a lieutenant colonel, with the Distinguished Service Cross with Oak Leaf Cluster, the *Croix de Guerre* with four palms and two stars, and had been made a *Chevalier de la Légion d'Honneur*.

On 30 April, the *Escadrille Lafayette's* non-identical twin children parted company as the 103rd Aero Squadron was detached from GC21 and sent to Bray Dunes to assist the British over Flanders. On 21 May Baer, in concert with 1Lts Herbert Wilcox, Hobart A H Baker and Chris Ford, brought down an Albatros west of Ypres. It was Baer's eighth victory and Ford's second.

The following day Baer was leading Lts Wilcox, Turnure, Dugan and Ernest A Giroux on a patrol when they encountered five German fighters south of Armentières. As the Americans dived on them, they were in turn jumped by three more Albatros D Vas of *Jasta* 18, which had been waiting for them to do just that. Giroux was shot down and killed by Ltn Hans Müller. Baer claimed an Albatros in flames, but he was in turn shot down by Gftr Deberitz and crash-landed near Laventie, suffering a broken knee in the process. He was then taken prisoner. Dugan, Turnure and Wilcox escaped the trap only with great difficulty.

The 103rd lost more *Lafayette* personnel when 1Lt Dugan was reassigned to Orly as a despatching officer on 31 May, and Capts Bridgman and Hill were transferred to the 139th Aero Squadron on 6 June. Two days later 1Lt Jones was ordered back to the United States to serve as an instructor and test pilot. He received a star to his *Croix de Guerre* on 17 November 1918, and would later be awarded the *Légion d'Honneur*. Post-war years, Hank Jones worked for the Pennsylvania Railroad, Transcontinental Air Transport-Maddux Air Lines and finally the F W Woolworth Company as a store manager until his retirement in 1960. He died in Clearwater, Florida, on 29 March 1972.

The 103rd Aero Squadron's SPADs are ready to return to action, with USAS roundels and rudder markings, as well as squadron insignia restored. Initially, however, the American unit fought on with French GC21, alongside SPA124, reconstituted with French personnel! (*George H Williams Collection via Greg VanWyngarden*)

Robert Soubiran's SPAD VII S3198 has had the Sioux head removed, but retains its French markings and his personal livery. The aeroplane was to undergo at least two markings changes while Soubiran flew it with the 103rd Aero Squadron between February and May 1918 (*Jack Eder Collection via Jon Guttman*)

On 29 June 1918, the 103rd Aero Squadron moved to Vaucouleurs, where, together with the 13th, 22nd and 139th Aero Squadrons, it formed the new 2nd Pursuit Group. All three squadrons were equipping and training on the SPAD XIII, equipped with the 220-hp geared Hispano-Suiza 8Be engine and twin Vickers machine guns. By the time they resumed combat operations on 11 July, the 103rd had come fully under the auspices of the USAS, which compelled the squadron to conform to a uniform system of markings. The old personal markings of the unit's *Lafayette* days were replaced by yellow numbers.

On 29 July Maj Thaw was given command of the 3rd Pursuit Group, comprising the 28th, 49th, 93rd and 213th Aero Squadrons, with Capt Bob Soubiran as his operations officer. On the same day, Capt Robert Rockwell assumed command of the 103rd Aero Squadron and 1Lt Ford was transferred to the 213th Aero Squadron. Thaw appealed to the 2nd Pursuit Group commander, Maj Davenport Johnson, to put his old squadron in the 3rd Pursuit, and on 6 August he duly traded the 49th for the 103rd. Soon after that, Thaw, emulating GC12's storks and

GC21's coloured bands – adopted variations on the 103rd's Indian head motif for the 3rd Pursuit's other squadrons, the 28th, 93rd and 213th.

Although few of its original *Lafayette* members remained – their experience was needed elsewhere throughout the USAS – the 103rd Aero Squadron retained the aggressive spirit of its predecessor, accounting for a total of 49 enemy aeroplanes. Ford rejoined the 103rd on 1 October, but the last of the old *Lafayette* men to contribute to the squadron tally was Carl Dolan during a dogfight with seven blue-tailed Fokker D VIIs on 12 October.

Observing a Fokker on the tail of his flight leader, 1Lt G DeFreest Larner, Dolan fired 100 rounds at long range before his guns jammed. After clearing them, he attacked three Fokkers that he saw chasing another SPAD, firing 100 rounds into one and seeing it fall away in a dive. The fighter was later reported to have crashed between Fontaine and Haraumont. A second Fokker was claimed in the same area by 1Lt Joseph Waddell.

Four days after finally getting a confirmed victory, Dolan was ordered to Washington, DC to serve as an advisor on pursuit work at the Office of the Director of Military Aeronautics. Later, he and Maj David Peterson got an assignment to Carlstrom and Door Field at Arcadia, Florida, where Dolan was put on the control board and served as the engineering officer.

Ford was leading a patrol on 15 October when he was hit by ground fire and forced to land at Remonville. While a prisoner, he was promoted to captain on 6 November. In spite of the Armistice, he was still in the prison camp at Villingen on 20 November, so he and some other impatient PoWs 'escaped'. After travelling 100 kilometres through the Black Forest and swimming the Rhine to France, Ford reached Colmar and rejoined the 103rd on 27 November. Made CO of the 213th Aero Squadron on 6 January 1919, Ford had been promoted to major by the time he returned to Boston on 12 July.

Another colourful SPA124 SPAD that carried on in the 103rd was 1Lt Chris Ford's machine, resplendent in his red, white and blue 'lightning' pattern personal livery (*Lafayette Foundation*)

A close-up of Ford's SPAD VII of the 103rd Aero Squadron at La Noblette in March 1918. The last American to join SPA124, Ford scored two victories in USAS service before being shot down and taken prisoner on 15 October 1918 (*Lafayette Foundation*)

Carl Dolan poses in the uniform of a first lieutenant in the USAS at the time of SPA124's transition to an American squadron at La Noblette in February 1918
(*Lafayette Foundation*)

Capt Robert Soubiran, commander of the 103rd Aero Squadron, with his Kellner-built SPAD XIII S7714. As CO of the unit, Soubiran continued to indulge in flamboyantly individualistic markings, including red diamonds on the tailplane and a red 'S' on the upper wing, instead of the more regulation yellow numeral
(*Greg VanWyngarden*)

He remained in the US Army Air Corps, but when it marked Col Ford as one of 385 officers to be removed from flying status, he chose to retire from the service on 31 March 1942. He then served as assistant chief inspector for the Consolidated Vultee plant in Miami, Florida, but died of cancer on 9 April 1945.

On 18 October 1918 'Doc' Rockwell was relieved of command for a rules infraction. Capt Soubiran took over the 103rd for the rest of the war, while Rockwell commanded the 93rd Aero Squadron. After his discharge, the French made Rockwell a *Chevalier de la Légion d'Honneur* on 17 May 1919. He worked for the Texas Company until 1921, then took up farming until 1928, when he directed the Emry-Riddle Company's flying school. Rockwell remained in the US Army Reserve, and in 1939 he returned to regular Army Air Corps service, serving throughout World War 2 as a colonel. After retiring from military service, he enrolled at the University of Redlands, California, under the GI Bill, and earned a degree in genealogy in 1953. Robert L Rockwell died of a heart attack in San Bernardino, California, on 25 January 1958.

Following the armistice, Robert Soubiran was made a *Chevalier de la Légion d'Honneur* on 9 April 1919, and a second palm was added to his *Croix de Guerre*.

Promoted to major and assigned to Langley Field after the war, Soubiran was unable to adjust to the peacetime Army and left it in 1919. Returning to Paris, he had a successful career as a salesman, and in 1940 he worked in the inspection department of Carl Dolan's Wissahickton Tool Works. During World War 2, Soubiran served as an aviation parts inspector in Connecticut for the War Assets Administration, and for Republic Aircraft in Farmingdale, New York. A heart condition forced him to retire, and he died in Queens, New York. on 4 February 1949. He left behind a wealth of historic photographs which his French-born wife, Anne-Marie Choudey Soubiran, donated to the National Air and Space Museum in Washington, DC prior to her death on 10 March 1982.

VOLUNTEERS FOR JEANNE D'ARC

Although it ceased to be an American squadron after February 1918, SPA124 continued to operate with foreign airmen on its rolls, some of whom were volunteers and some of whom were temporarily assigned – the latter including one more American. Among the flying personnel slated for the new French squadron on 17 December 1917 were three Portuguese army officers, Capitaines Santos Leite and Antonio de Souza Maya, and Lt Alberto Lello Portela.

The one who would serve longest, Lello Portela, had been born in Fontes on 10 June 1893, and joined the 23rd Infantry Regiment of the Portuguese army on 24 April 1911. He trained to be a cavalryman until 1914, and in 1915 he took pilot training at Pau and Cazaux. After Portugal entered the war in 1917, he, Souza Maya and Leite were assigned to SPA124. By then, Leite had also seen some action in November with No 10 Sqn, Royal Flying Corps.

Czech volunteer Václav Pilát stands before a Sopwith 1¹/₂ Strutter of _escadrille_ Sop9 prior to his transfer to SPA124 (_Radko Vasicek Collection via Jon Guttman_)

Another foreign member on the 17 December roll was Wenceslas Pilat, one of eight Czechs and one Slovak whose very presence in French service would have earned them death sentences for treason had they been captured by the Germans.

Born in Bohemia on 14 March 1889, Václav Pilát had studied engineering in Prague until 1913, then moved to Paris and was working in a cosmetic factory when war broke out. Although an Austro-Hungarian citizen, Pilát believed that an Allied victory might break up the Hapsburg empire, leading to Czech independence. He therefore enlisted in the Foreign Legion on 24 August and was assigned to the *Bataillon* Nazdar, made up of 300 Czech volunteers.

Wounded in the leg near Reims in January 1915, Pilát decided to transfer into aviation. After earning his *brevet* at Pau on 27 March 1916, he was assigned to C104, flying photoreconnaissance missions over Verdun and Soissons. He also became involved in espionage in the autumn of 1916 when he also inserted a French soldier in civilian clothing behind German lines in the Alsace-Lorraine sector. Later, he requested reassignment to fighters, and after training on Nieuports and SPAD VIIs, he joined SPA124.

There was one other *Lafayette* remnant in SPA124 in the form of the older unit's third executive officer, Lt Louis Verdier-Fauvety. About a month after formation, however, he transferred to SPA163. Verdier scored three victories and was given command of his old unit, SPA65, when he was killed during a German night bombardment on 21 August 1918. His good friend, and fellow N124 alumnus, Charles Nungesser

Lt Alberto Lello Portela, one of two Portuguese pilots assigned to SPA124, poses beside his de Marcay-built SPAD VII (S5721) in May 1918. (*Marcel Robert album via Jon Guttman*)

devoted himself to avenging his death thereafter, applying the legend *Lt. Verdier* under the cockpit of his SPAD XIII for the rest of the war.

SPA124 got off to a discouraging start when Sous-Lts Gaston Rousset and Henri Vimal du Monteil collided in mid-air over Saint Étienne au Temple while returning from a patrol on 17 March. Nobody could have suspected at the time that they would be the *escadrille's* only fatalities for the rest of the war. A short while later Leite was badly injured when his SPAD flipped over on landing as he returned from a mission.

He and Souza Maya left SPA124 in April, but Lello Portela stayed on, proudly proclaiming Portugal's presence over the Western Front by painting pennants and a medallion based on the national flag over the white fuselage band of his SPAD VII, S5721. In May SPA124 got another foreign volunteer, this time from Russia.

Born in the Crimean city of Yalta on 1 March 1887, Pavel Vladimirovich Argeyev was a lieutenant colonel in the Imperial Russian Army who happened to be in France when war broke out. Resigning his Russian commission, he enlisted in the Foreign Legion on 12 September 1914. Lt Argeyev – or Paul d'Argueeff, as the French spelled it – was made a *Chevalier de la Légion d'Honneur* for valour under fire, but two wounds led to his being declared unfit for infantry duty, at which point he transferred into aviation.

After training, Capitaine Argeyev joined N48 on 1 June 1916, but in mid-July he was sent to the Eastern Front and assigned to the 1st Fighter Group, Imperial Russian Air Service, led by Rotmistr Aleksandr A Kozakov. There, he was credited with six German aircraft destroyed between 27 February and 21 June 1917. Following the Revolution, and the signing of the Treaty of Brest-Litovsk by the Bolsheviks, Argeyev returned to France in April 1918 and joined SPA124 on 11 May.

SPA124's first official victory was a Rumpler destroyed over Saint Souplet by Adjutant Paul Bentejac and Sgt Marcel Chöel on 14 May. The end of May saw GC21 supporting the I Colonial Corps as it defended Reims against the latest wave in the Germans' spring offensive. On the

This line-up of SPA124 SPAD VIIs in May 1918 includes aircraft '19', flown by Russian volunteer Capitaine Pavel Argeyev (*SHAA B87.3781*)

SPAD VIIs of French SPA124, using a white band as the new unit insignia, line up at La Noblette in March 1918. The machine at left, with the letter *H* on a cross, was flown by the *escadrille* commander, Lt André d'Humières, while aircraft '3' was flown by Sous-Lt Marcel Robert (*SHAA B87.3779*)

Another SPA124 line-up photograph taken in May 1918, this shot includes (from left) the SPAD VII of Adjutant Pilát, the SPAD XIII of Sous-Lt Robert and (at right) the SPAD XIII of Sous-Lt Henri Barancy (*Radko Vasicek Collection via Jon Guttman*)

31st, Lt Lello Portela and Adjutant Pilát were cited for assisting Capitaine d'Humières in the burning of a balloon near Saint Thierry, while Italian front veteran Lt Marcel Robert sent an enemy scout down to crash near Prouilly for his second victory and Lt Henri Barancy downed a two-seater over Branscourt. Barancy shot down a German fighter on 1 June, while Argeyev reopened his account with the destruction of an enemy aeroplane over Pusieux-Beaumont.

Cpl Louis Charton was shot down in flames during a fight with 12 enemy fighters over La Pompelle that day, but he jettisoned his burning fuel tank and crash-landed, wounded but alive.

After the front around Reims stabilised, GC21 was moved from the *IVème* to the *VIème Armée* sector, ultimately settling at Francheville, near the front at Villers-Cotterets and Dormans. In recognition of his squadron's distinguished record in the Reims' defence, Capitaine d'Humières authorised the addition of a helmeted bust of Jeanne d'Arc,

This group photograph of GC21 pilots includes, from left to right, Lt Henri Barancy (SPA124), Capitaine Henri Nompére de Champagny (commander of SPA163) and Capitaine Pavel Argeyev, who added nine victories with SPA124 to the previous six he had scored over his native Russia. Sous-Lt Marcel Robert of SPA124 is in the foreground, playing with the dog (*SHAA B87.3846*)

based on a statue at the Cathedral of Frémiet, over the white fuselage band as a unit marking.

On 4 June Pilát got into a fight with nine Fokker Dr I triplanes, and after driving one down he managed to escape the rest by putting his SPAD XIII (S2809) into a steep dive, but whilst pulling out he was struck in the leg by a bullet from below. He may have been credited to Ltn Heinrich Drekmann of *Jasta* 4, but he made it to Allied lines and was hospitalised.

Argeyev kept adding to his score in June – a Rumpler on the 13th, followed by two-seaters the next day and on the 26th, raising his total to ten. 'Capitaine Argeyev wasn't a refined pilot', recalled one of his squadronmates, then-Sous-Lt Marcel Robert. 'Very rough in his piloting, but an extraordinary warrior and hunter. He only liked to fly and fight alone. Considering his background, our squadron commander left him entirely free to fly when and as he pleased. Being of Slavic temperament, he had fits of passivity, sometimes waiting numerous days to just watch us fly, or sleep in the sun. Then, when the fit passed, he would leave alone to hunt. Argeyev had the "eye of the hunter" to an extraordinary degree, discovering game when we couldn't find it. As soon as an adversary revealed himself, he would charge at full speed, diving to break everything, without making the slightest manoeuvre, and would not fire until he had closed to point-blank range. And thus, he had more victories than any of us over *"l'idioteBoche"*, as Argeyev called the enemy'.

On 29 July Lello Portela left SPA124. He was made a *Chevalier de la Légion d'Honneur* and also awarded the *Croix de Guerre* with palm by the French, to which Portugal would add the *Cruz de Guerra 1a Classe* on 26 March 1919. In later years Lello Portela served as Prefect of Lisbon. He died on 10 October 1949.

The day after Lello Portela departed, his replacement arrived in the person of 1Lt Henry B Marsh, on assignment from the USAS. The first

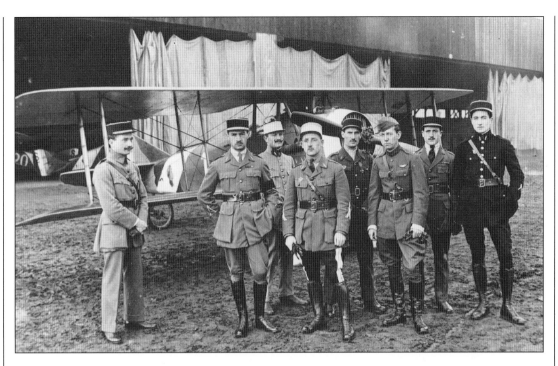

American to serve in SPA124 since February, Marsh would fly 16 combat patrols and three reconnaissance missions by the end of the war. SPA124 underwent a change of command on 9 August, when d'Humières was promoted to greater responsibilities and Lt Henri Bergé took charge. Bergé had previously scored one victory with SPA92, and would be credited with three more while leading SPA124.

After another 'dry spell', Argeyev resumed his scoring with a Fokker D VII on 27 September, and two two-seaters the next day. The 28th also saw the return of Adjutant Pilát, who, after recovering from his wound, had served for a time in the newly formed SPA164, before returning to his old outfit. Argeyev downed two more two-seaters on 5 and 30 October 1918. The latter was his last victory, as well as the 26th, and last, for SPA124 since its return to combat as a French squadron, for the loss of two pilots killed in accidents and, remarkably, none lost in action.

The French SPA124 had done its American forebear proud, but curiously only two pilots had achieved acedom while flying in the squadron in either incarnation, and both were foreign volunteers – Raoul Lufbery with 16 and Pavel Argeyev, who scored nine of his 15 victories with SPA124.

After the war, Argeyev joined the Compagnie Franco-Romaine, flying the commercial route between Prague, in Czechoslovakia, and Warsaw, in Poland, but on 30 October 1922 he became disoriented in bad weather and perished when his aircraft crashed into a mountain near Trutnow, on the German-Czechoslovakian border.

By the time Vacláv Pilát was demobilised in 1919, he had received the *Médaille Militaire* and the *Croix de Guerre* with two palms and two stars for his service to France. In September he returned to the newly formed Republic of Czechoslovakia, which subsequently awarded him the *Válecny Kriz* and the *Revolucni Medaile*. Pilát died in 1979 at the age of 90.

These pilots of SPA124 at Bourget aerodrome in November 1918 include, from left to right, Adjutant Pilát, Sous-Lt Louis Douillet, unidentified, Capitaine Henri Bergé (SPA124's last commander), Adjutant Paul Bentejac, 2Lt Henry B Marsh (USAS) and Adjutants Salah Simer and Emmanuele Corso (*Radko Vasicek Collection via Jon Guttman*)

LAFAYETTE POSTSCRIPT

Many members of the *Escadrille Lafayette* were either still in the unit or still in France when it was transformed into the 103rd Aero Squadron, but most of them were dispersed among other outfits. Their combat experience made them invaluable to the USAS fighter squadrons that were forming up at Toul in the spring of 1918, but the *Lafayette* men had had little or no exposure to US Army standards of training and discipline, and that sometimes necessitated some mental adjustment on one or the other party's part.

Remarkably – but not too surprisingly – the USAS did not know quite what to do with Raoul Lufbery. At first it assigned him to the Aviation Instruction Centre at Issoudun, expecting him to write books on combat tactics. On 18 February, however, he was transferred to the 95th Aero Squadron at Villeneuve des Vertus to teach its personnel in a more hands-on manner. On 5 March the 94th Aero Squadron arrived on the airfield, and Lufbery trained pilots of both units.

The squadrons were equipped with the Nieuport 28.C1, a biplane powered by a 160-hp Gnome monosoupape rotary engine and armed with twin 0.30-cal Vickers machine guns. Only enough guns had arrived

Lufbery beside his Nieuport 28 N6193 of the 94th Aero Squadron. He flew 2Lt Philip W Davis' Nieuport N6178 in his last combat of 19 May 1918. Ironically, Davis was in Lufbery's N6193 when he was shot down and killed on 2 June – by the same German who had claimed Jimmy Hall, Ltn Friedrich Hengst of *Jasta* 64w (*Greg VanWyngarden*)

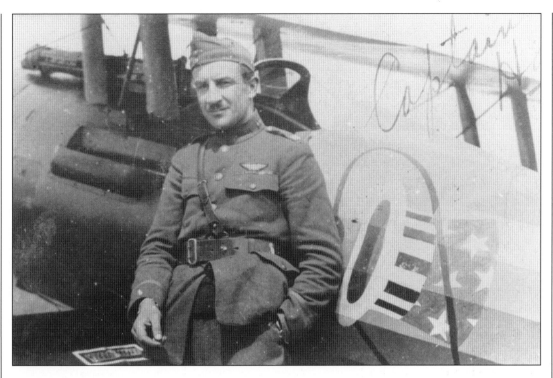

Sporting a moustache, Capt James N Hall strikes a typical pose beside his Nieuport 28 of the 94th Aero Squadron in April 1918 (*Greg VanWyngarden*)

to mount one per aeroplane, however, and they had yet to be installed. Disgusted at the slowness with which his countrymen were going into action, 'Luf' led the 94th's first patrol in an unarmed aircraft, his 'lucky' wingmen being 1Lts Douglas Campbell and Edward V Rickenbacker.

The 94th also had the benefit of some other ex-*Lafayette* men, namely Jimmy Hall, Dave Peterson and Kenneth Marr. Doug Campbell and 2Lt Alan F Winslow – the latter a *Lafayette* Flying Corps volunteer with previous service in SPA152 – scored the 94th's first victories by bringing down an Albatros D Va and a Pfalz D IIIa of Royal Würtemburg *Jasta* 64 on 14 April. On the 29th Hall and Rickenbacker drove down another *Jasta* 64w Pfalz – Hall's fourth victory, and the first of an eventual 26 for the future American ace of aces.

During a fight on 3 May, former LFC pilot 2Lt Charles W Chapman was shot down in flames by Oblt Erwin Wenig, commander of Bavarian *Jasta* 80, who was then driven down in a dive by Capt Peterson. Wenig survived, but in the confusion of the aerial melée other 94th pilots mistook Chapman's falling aeroplane for his, and credited Peterson with downing the German in flames.

On 7 May Hall, Rickenbacker and 1Lt M Edwin Green took on three of *Jasta* 64w's aircraft, during which Ltn Friedrich Hengst got on Hall's tail. As the American tried to dive away, the fabric on his upper wing tore off – a frequent flaw on the Nieuport 28 at that time – and his engine was hit by a shell from *M. Flak* 57, causing him to crash land, breaking his nose (again) and at least one ankle. In spite of the circumstances surrounding his capture, Hall was credited to Hengst, and while waiting to be taken away as a PoW, his hosts at *Jasta* 64w told him that in that same fight one of their members, Ltn Wilhelm Scheerer, had crash-landed with a stomach wound from he died a few hours later. After his release from

109

Hall takes off from Gengoult aerodrome, near Toul, in his Nieuport 28 N6153. On 29 April he scored his fourth victory, in concert with 1Lt Edward V Rickenbacker, but on 7 May Hall was brought down, injured and taken prisoner. Although credited to Ltn Friedrich Hengst of Royal Würtemburg *Jasta* 64w, Hall believed his aeroplane to have been a victim of anti-aircraft fire from the ground (*George H. Williams Collection, via Jon Guttman*)

Lanshut prison, Hall reported Scheerer's loss, which was belatedly credited to Rickenbacker.

Hall was awarded the *Croix de Guerre* with five palms, the *Médaille Militaire* and *Légion d'Honneur*, as well as the DFC, but his greatest fame lay ahead. Hall's uncompleted book, *High Adventure*, was published after he was shot down. That influenced Dr Gros to ask him to edit a history of the *Lafayette* Flying Corps in collaboration with LFC member and SPA99 veteran Charles Bernard Nordhoff. Upon first meeting with his aloof, fastidious associate, the first thought to cross the outgoing Hall's mind was, 'Lord! How am I going to work with this man?' But it proved to be the beginning of a successful 28-year literary team-up.

After the publication of their two-volume *History of the Lafayette Flying Corps* in 1920, the duo went to Tahiti and wrote *Fairy Lands of the South Seas*, published in 1921. After a dry spell, they produced *Falcons of France* in 1929, then between 1932 and 1934 they wrote their most famous work, the *Bounty* Trilogy – *Mutiny on the Bounty*, *Men Against the Sea*, and *Pitcairn's Island*. That was followed by *The Hurricane* and *Botany Bay*, but Nordhoff was falling into alcoholism and deteriorating health. The next novel, *Men Without a Country*, was mostly Hall's work, and *The High Barbaree* was completely Hall's, although he still shared the by-line and royalties with his friend.

After Nordhoff died of a heart attack on 11 April 1947, Hall continued writing, and was nearing the completion of his autobiography when he too died of a heart attack on 6 July 1951 on the isle of Papeete, in Tahiti. He was buried on a hillside facing Mavati Bay, where HMS *Bounty* had first dropped anchor.

Marr had a close call on 10 May, when his Nieuport and that of 1Lt Thorne Taylor's collided on Gengoult airfield. Their wings locked together and the firing mechanism of Marr's machine guns jammed down, resulting in both planes spinning around like 'a gigantic pin wheel', as Rickenbacker described it, spraying bullets in all directions until Marr's weapons either ran out of ammunition or jammed.

Capt David Peterson beside a Nieuport 28 of B Flight of the 94th Aero Squadron on 17 May 1918. Peterson commanded A Flight in the 94th from 1 April to 25 May 1918, then flew in the 95th Aero Squadron, adding five victories to the one he had scored with the *Escadrille Lafayette* (*Greg VanWyngarden*)

Peterson was credited with two more victories on 15 May, and was transferred to the 95th Aero Squadron the next day. No sooner had he arrived than he scored his fifth victory over a two-seater near St Mihiel on the 17th. He downed another enemy two-seater on 20 May, and was given command of the 95th on the 22nd. Promoted to major on 29 August, Peterson was ordered home to serve as an instructor on 8 October.

Later, he and Carl Dolan served in Arcadia, Florida, and on 16 March 1919 Peterson and Lt F X Paversick were flying a new dual-control D 9 aeroplane over Daytona Beach when it went into an uncontrollable climb – Paversick had accidentally locked his control column into a snap-lock socket. Before Paversick could unlock his joystick, the aeroplane stalled and came down tail-first. The engine broke loose from its mount, crushing Peterson to death. Paversick died of his injuries shortly after.

Six days later Dolan, Hank Jones and pilots from the 95th Aero Squadron carried David Peterson's casket to its final resting place at the Glen Dyberry Cemetery in Homesdale, Pennsylvania. The populace of

Former *Lafayette* Flying Corps member Maj John Huffer, commander of the 94th Aero Squadron, USAS, shares some thoughts with Maj Lufbery, who he selected as his operations officer to make the most of Lufbery's wealth of combat experience for the benefit of new pilots (*Greg VanWyngarden*)

his hometown resisted efforts to have his body reinterred in the *Lafayette Escadrille* memorial in 1928, and Peterson's tomb there remains empty.

Among the most dramatic losses to the *Escadrille Lafayette* occurred on 19 May 1918, three months after the unit had disbanded. It began when a Rumpler from the *Reihenbildtrupp* (long-range picture section) of *Armee Abteilung C*, flown by Gftr Otto Kirschbaum and Ltn Kurt Scheibe, crossed the lines, eliciting responses from both French *escadrille* SPA68 and the 94th Aero Squadron.

First to take off was 1Lt Oscar J Gude, who attacked the Germans at a hopelessly long range until his ammunition was used up. Majs Lufbery and John Huffer took off five minutes later, and and the former made two attacks before Scheibe's return fire apparently severed a control wire or even his stick, causing the Nieuport to go into a sudden roll. Lufbery, who in his haste to take off may not have fastened his seat belt, was thrown from his aeroplane and fell on a garden fence near the village of Maron.

Pressing their luck, the Germans turned back to resume their mission, only to be attacked by SPADs from SPA68. This time Scheibe's return fire struck Adjutant Pierre Baudry in the heart, but then Sgt Dupré forced the Rumpler down near Flainval, where its crew was taken prisoner.

While engaging a Rumpler from the *Reihenbildtrupp* (long-range picture section) of *Armee Abteilung C*, flown by Gftr Otto Kirschbaum and Ltn Kurt Scheibe, Lufbery's Nieuport was hit and sent out of control. Thrown from his aeroplane, he struck this picket fence in Maron, just north of Nancy (*Greg VanWyngarden*)

At the time of his death, Lufbery was the leading American ace. His many decorations included the *Chevalier de la Légion d'Honneur*, *Médaille Militaire*, *Croix de Guerre* with ten palms and the British Military Cross. Although he was buried in the American Cemetery near the Sebastopol Woods on 20 May, his remains were later reinterred on 4 July 1928 in a crypt where they, of all the unit's members, most deserved to rest – in the *Lafayette Escadrille* Memorial.

An hour after Lufbery died, Douglas Campbell destroyed another Rumpler from F. Fl. Abt.(A) 298b near Flirey, killing Ltn Wilhelm Bayer and Ludwig Kammerer. And on that same day one of Lufbery's *Lafayette* squadronmates, Adjutant Edwin Parsons, by then flying with SPA3, downed a two-seater at Montdidier in concert with Maréchal-des-Logis Jules Denneulin and Sgt Maurice Chevannes, killing Uffz Walter Graaf

The day after his death at age 33, Lufbery received a full military funeral at near Toul, with his former commander in the Philippines, Maj Gen Clarence R Edwards – now commanding the 26th Infantry Division – delivering the eulogy (*Greg VanWyngarden*)

Flowers cover Lufbery's coffin after the funeral. His body was laid to rest in the American Cemetery at Sebastopol Barracks. It was reinterred in the *Lafayette Escadrille* Memorial on 4 July 1928 (*Greg VanWyngarden*)

and Sgt Christian Hofele. As a man who lived for vengeance, Lufbery might have appreciated how soon his own had been arranged, but the loss of expertise that his death represented to the USAS might be gauged from the success of the 94th Aero Squadron and the aces he had mentored, such as Doug Campbell, James Meissner and Eddie Rickenbacker.

The passive role played by Huffer during Lufbery's last combat may have led to his being transferred to command the 93rd Aero Squadron on 9 June, and command of the 94th being given to Kenneth Marr. The latter was promoted to major on 17 September, but his health had been undermined by his previous gassing and injuries, and on the 25th Rickenbacker succeeded him as the 94th's commander. After the war, Marr worked at Paramount Pictures as an assistant to director John Ford,

Capt Robert L Rockwell as commander of the 93rd Aero Squadron with his Kellner-built SPAD XIII, S4541 (*Jon Guttman*)

1Lts Edward V Rickenbacker and Douglas Campbell join Capt Ken Marr before a Nieuport 28 of B Flight, 94th Aero Squadron, with white painted cowling and part of the propeller. Marr led the squadron from 9 June to 25 September 1918, when Rickenbacker succeeded him (*Greg VanWyngarden*)

Lafayette **Flying Corps ace 1Lt David E Putnam and Capt Dudley Hill, shown at Toul on 18 July 1918, lent their experience to the 139th Aero Squadron during its combat debut that month (*Jon Guttman*)**

Although he had developed an aversion to war, Capt Ray C Bridgman dutifully led the 22nd Aero Squadron in 1918 (*Lafayette Foundation*)

and went on to succeed in several business ventures before retiring to Phoenix, Arizona. Marr died of arteriosclerosis in Palo Alto, California, on 28 December 1963.

Two *Lafayette* alumni lent their experience to the 2nd Pursuit Group when Capts Ray Bridgman and Dudley Hill were transferred from the 103rd to the 139th Aero Squadron on 6 June 1918. Although pleased to be flying the SPAD XIII, Bridgman was morose to learn that his friend Jimmy Hall was a German prisoner, and still wrote of conflicting feelings about the war in general. 'The world is now a slaughter house. He who slaughters most is honoured more than a poet or a Christ'. Nonetheless, on 10 August Bridgman officially joined the slaughter when he and 1Lt Vaughn R McCormick shot down a Rumpler two-seater over Xivray. Five days later, Bridgman was placed in command of the 2nd Pursuit Group's youngest outfit, the 22nd Aero Squadron.

On 12 September the American Expeditionary Force launched its first major operation of the war, as Gen John J Pershing's 19 divisions fell upon the ten withdrawing divisions of Gen Max von Gallwitz's *Armee Gruppe C* in the St Mihiel salient. Seven hours into the offensive, Bridgman sent a Hannover CL III down out of control, but was then himself brought down by ground fire just behind German lines, although he managed to make it to safety in Allied territory.

Bridgman scored his second confirmed victory on 22 September, and on the 24th he shared in downing a DFW C V near Woel with 1Lts Raymond J Little and Harold B Hudson. On 28 September the 22nd got into a chaotic battle royal during which two Fokker D VIIs were credited to 1Lt Clinton Jones, one each to 1Lts Henry Hudson and Frank B Tyndall, one was shared by 1Lts Jacques M Swaab and James D Beane, and a sixth shared by Bridgman and 1Lt Watson W LaForce. It was Bridgman's fourth credited victory. Although he did not 'make ace', he led the 22nd to become the highest-scoring squadron in the 2nd Pursuit Group with a total of 42 victories.

After returning quietly from the front, Bridgman completed his studies at Yale and taught European History at New York University. Still haunted by the war, he became an ardent pacifist. The outbreak of World War 2, and the participation of his sons in it, caused him further pain,

Capt Bridgman poses beside his SPAD XIII S18815. During the course of leading the 22nd Aero Squadron, he was credited with four victories (*Jon Guttman*)

although the post-war creation of the United Nations renewed his hopes. Amid the Korean War, however, Bridgman developed phlebitis and pneumonia and eschewed medical attention. On 9 November 1951 Ray Bridgman fell – or, perhaps more likely, jumped – from the Staten Island Ferry and drowned.

On 1 August 1918 Capt Hill left the 139th to take command of the newly formed 138th Aero Squadron, although that unit still had yet to enter combat when he was promoted to command of the 5th Pursuit Group on 1 November. Discharged in March 1919, Hill had had enough of flying and pursued a number of occupations – including a job at Carl Dolan's Wissahickon Tool Works – before dying of a heart attack in Peekskill, New York, on 30 June 1951.

While other *Lafayette* pilots were having mixed fortunes in the USAS, Lt(sg) Willis Haviland took command of the US Naval Air Station at Porto Corsini on 23 July 1918. Equipped with 35 Macchi flying boats, the unit's primary mission was to patrol the Adriatic Sea and engage units from the Austro-Hungarian naval bases at Trieste and Pola.

However, Haviland was soon at odds with the commander of US Naval Forces in Italy, Lt Cdr John L Callan, who did not share Haviland's belief that commanding officers should fly missions. After watching his men return from a mission with their aircraft riddled, he led the next patrol and plunged into a formation of fighters from Pola. Haviland subsequently became the first American to bomb Pola by night, while Callan threatened to relieve him of command. Told that he would be court-martialled for leading his men in disobedience of orders, Haviland replied, 'I wasn't leading my men – I was too far ahead of them for that'.

In spite of Callan's objections, Haviland's leadership by example seems to have made NAS Porto Corsini the most combat-active air station in the US Navy. One member, Charles H Hammann, was awarded the Medal of Honor, and 14 others received the Navy Cross, including Haviland. By the end of the war, Haviland's honours would also include the French *Croix de Guerre* with two palms and two star, the Belgian *Croix de Guerre* with palm and the Italian *Croce di Guerra* and *Medaglia Militare*.

Haviland stayed in the Navy until his discharge as a lieutenant commander on 27 December 1925. He had a successful business career thereafter, but following the Japanese attack on Pearl Harbor on 7 December 1941 – in which two battleships on which he had served, the USS *Arizona* and USS *Oklahoma*, were sunk – he rejoined the Navy as a commander. In September 1944, however, he fell ill with what x-rays revealed to be a lung tumour. After undergoing surgery at the US Naval Hospital in Corona, California, Willis Haviland developed pneumonia and died on 27 November.

While so many of his colleagues joined the USAS – with a variety of results – on 24 April 1918 Edwin Parsons was assigned to SPA3, attached to GC12 'Les Cigognes'. This was the highest-scoring and most famous *escadrille* in the *Service Aeronautique*, its past members including such heroes as André Chainat, Albert Deullin, Alfred Heurteaux, René Dorme, Alfred Auger, Mathieu Tenant de la Tour and Georges Guynemer. Since Guynemer's death on 11 September 1917, SPA3 was virtually a different squadron, with a new generation of pilots keen to emulate their renowned forebears. It was no environment in which to rest on one's *Lafayette* laurels, and Parsons had no intention of doing so.

On 6 May Parsons reopened his account by downing a two-seater. Three days later, he and Sgt Frank Leaman Baylies (an LFC volunteer from New Bedford, Massachusetts) bet a bottle of champagne that they could shoot down an enemy aeroplane before Sous-Lt René Fonck, the highly skilled but overbearing top ace of neighbouring *escadrille* SPA103. Baylies brought down a Halberstadt CL II over German lines between Braches and Gratibus, but Fonck asked that the wager be altered to favour whoever downed the most enemy aeroplanes that day. The Americans reluctantly agreed, and Fonck went on to shoot down six that afternoon.

Parsons downed a two-seater on 16 May, destroyed another on the 19th and became an ace by disposing of yet another two-seater the next day. Baylies had been scoring at a steadier rate, bringing his tally to 12 on 31 May – and making him SPA3's leading ace of 1918.

On 17 June, however, Baylies was leading Maréchal-des-Logis André Dubonnet and Sgt François Macari on patrol when they spotted a higher formation of four rotary-engined aeroplanes that they assumed to be British Sopwiths. They turned out to be Fokker Dr Is of *Jasta* 19, one of which, probably flown by Ltn Rudolf Rienau, shot Baylies down in flames near Rollot, while another, flown by Ltn Wilhelm Leusch, sent Dubonnet crash-landing in Allied lines. In 1928 Baylies' body was reinterred in the *Escadrille Lafayette* memorial.

Preferring to remain in French service, Edwin Parsons served out the rest of World War 1 with the famous *escadrille* SPA3 'Les Cigognes', scoring a total of eight victories. In 1940 he joined the US Navy as a lieutenant commander, rising to rear admiral by 1945 (*Jon Guttman*)

On 26 August Parsons avenged Baylies by shooting down a Fokker D VII. When Capitaine Georges Raymond had to relinquish his command of SPA3 due to pneumonia – which would cause his death on 4 October – Sous-Lt Parsons took acting leadership of the *escadrille* for a time. Parsons teamed up with Maréchal-des-Logis Denneulin and Sous-Lt Pierre Pendaries of SPA67 to destroy a two-seater south of Tahure on 26 September, and scored a solo success over another two-seater on 1 October. Only two aces were still with SPA3 when the war ended – Parsons with eight victories and André Dubonnet with six.

During the post-war years, Parsons worked as an agent for the Federal Bureau of Investigation and as a writer or advisor on several aviation films. He also wrote for pulp magazines, published a book on his wartime experiences and wrote and narrated a 15-minute radio series, *Heroes of the Lafayette*. In 1940, Parsons joined the US Navy as a lieutenant commander, served in the Solomon Islands and had risen to the rank of rear admiral by the end of World War 2. After receiving a rather overdue *Légion d'Honneur* in 1962, Edwin Parsons died on 2 May 1968, and is buried at Arlington National Cemetery.

Following his honourable discharge on 17 July 1919, Bill Thaw returned to Pittsburgh, where he became an agent for his father's General Insurance Company, and also involved himself in commercial aviation. In 1924, Dr Edmond Gros told Thaw of plans to erect a monument to the *Escadrille Lafayette*, but it led to a bitter struggle as Thaw fought Frederick Prince Snr's efforts to turn it into a memorial to Norman Prince, who his father persistently tried to represent as the sole founder of the unit. When the memorial was dedicated on 4 July 1928, it was for the entire *Lafayette* Flying Corps, but Thaw never got to join his comrades there. After succumbing to pneumonia on 22 April 1934, he was buried in the Allegheny Cemetery in Pittsburgh.

N124's commander, Georges Thenault, married an American, Sarah Spencer, and wrote a book on his old unit, *l'Escadrille Lafayette*. He left the air service in 1935 as a colonel to become president of the Ethyl Corporation for France, and in 1939 he, Dr Gros, Paul Rockwell and Harold Willis tried to convince the French government to form a new *Escadrille Lafayette* until the German invasion on 10 May 1940 curtailed their effort.

Sending his wife and two children to safety in the United States, Thenault sat out the war at home, to be reunited with them thereafter. He died of a cerebral haemorrhage on 17 December 1948, and was buried in the *Escadrille Lafayette* Memorial that he had helped to dedicate 20 years earlier.

Joining him are the six Americans who actually occupy the 12 crypts in the memorial installed for former *Escadrille Lafayette* members – James R Doolittle, Edmond Genet, Ronald Hoskier, Raoul Lufbery, Douglas MacMonagle and Paul Pavelka.

SPA124's teetotaller, Carl Dolan, had a long and eventful post-war life. After retiring from the USAS in 1920, with the *Croix de Guerre* and *Légion d'Honneur* for his wartime service, he was sent to China as an advisor to help that country develop its own military air arm. While en route, he met Ramona Frances Morgan, who he married in Beijing on 10 July 1921. Dolan trained fledgling Chinese pilots until 1925, then returned to

Carl Dolan gives yet another interview – this time with a French television news team – during the last international reunion of World War 1 aces in Paris in November 1981. It was his last chance to 'set the record straight', and to revisit the *Lafayette Escadrille* Monument, before his death on 31 December (*Jon Guttman*)

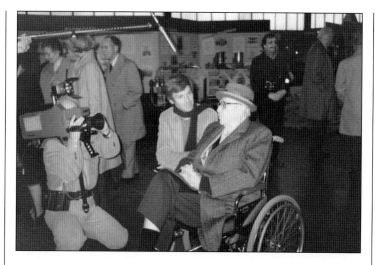

Hawaii, where he helped design John Rogers Field (now Honolulu International Airport). He subsequently became involved in numerous other businesses in and out of aviation, including Eastern Airlines, Wissahickon Tool Works Inc and, from 1943 to 1945, was president of Commonwealth Aircraft Company in Kansas City, Missouri, the second largest manufacturer of combat gliders during World War 2.

During the Korean War, Col Dolan was assistant to the chief of maintenance of the US Air Force at the headquarters of the Air Materiel Command at Wright-Patterson Air Force Base, Ohio. He was later the USAF representative, troubleshooter and consultant at the Sperry Corporation. By the time he retired to Hawaii, Dolan's achievements

Weathered but undergoing renovation, the *Lafayette Escadrille* Monument still honours France's American flying volunteers in February 2003 (*Jon Guttman*)

included the first insulated berths in aircraft, the first operational manual for airlines and some of the first instrument landing systems. He also helped to write the original charter for the Civil Aeronautics Administration.

A lifelong standard bearer for 'keeping the record straight' about the *Escadrille Lafayette,* Dolan represented the unit at numerous reunions and ceremonies. His last came in November 1981, when he was invited to an international reunion of surviving World War 1 aces in Paris. He was then 86, and had been diagnosed with lymphoma cancer, but he was not about to let this last honour go. He may have contracted pneumonia while visiting the *Lafayette Memorial* on 10 November, but in any case, shortly after returning to Honolulu, the last of the 38 Americans to fly in the *Escadrille Lafayette* died on 31 December 1981.

On 22 August 1985 Paul Rockwell, Kiffin's brother and elected historian of the *escadrille,* died in Asheville, North Carolina, aged 96. N124 now lives on only in memory, but even stripped of myth, it remains a vivid memory indeed.

A gathering of all 38 Americans who flew in N124 *Escadrille Lafayette* between April 1916 and February 1918 (*Charles H Dolan via Jon Guttman*)

APPENDICES

APPENDIX 1

ESCADRILLE N124 PERSONNEL, APRIL 1916-FEBRUARY 1918

Name	Joined N124	Victories	Departed	Remarks
Georges Thenault	20 April 1916	1	6 January 1918	Pau
Alfred de Laage de Meux	20 April 1916	3	23 May 1917	KIC
Victor E Chapman	20 April 1916	-	23 June 1916	KIA
Norman Prince	20 April 1916	3	12 October 1916	KIC
James R McConnell	20 April 1916	-	19 March 1917	KIA
Kiffin Y Rockwell	20 April 1916	3	23 September 1916	KIA
William Thaw	20 April 1916	2	18 February 1918	103rd AS
W Bert Hall	28 April 1916	3	1 November 1916	N103
Elliot C Cowdin	28 April 1916	-	25 June 1916	'Ill health'
G Raoul Lufbery	24 May 1916	16	5 January 1918	USAS
H Clyde Balsley	29 May 1916	-	18 June 1916	WIA
Charles C Johnson	29 May 1916	1	31 October 1917	Tours
Lawrence Rumsey	4 June 1916	-	25 November 1916	Ill health
Dudley L Hill	9 June 1916	-	18 February 1918	103rd AS
Didier Masson	19 June 1916	1	8 October 1917	-
Charles Nungesser	14 July 1916	1	15 August 1916	N65
Paul Pavelka	11 August 1916	-	24 January 1917	N391
Robert L Rockwell	17 September 1916	-	18 February 1918	103rd AS
Willis B Haviland	22 October 1916	1	18 September 1917	SPA102
Frederick H Prince Jnr	22 October 1916	-	15 February 1917	Pau
Robert Soubiran	22 October 1916	1	18 February 1918	103rd AS
Ronald W Hoskier	11 December 1916	-	23 April 1917	KIA
Edmond C C Genet	19 January 1917	-	16 April 1917	KIA
Edwin C Parsons	25 January 1917	1	26 February 1918	SPA3
Stephen Bigelow	8 February 1917	-	11 September 1917	WIA
Walter Lovell	26 February 1917	1	24 October 1917	Chaumont
Edward F Hinkle	1 March 1916	-	12 June 1917	-
Harold B Willis	1 March 1917	-	18 August 1917	POW
Kenneth Marr	29 March 1917	1	18 February 1918	103rd AS
William E Dugan Jnr	30 March 1917	-	18 February 1918	103rd AS
Thomas M Hewitt Jnr	30 March 1917	-	17 September 1917	Grounded
Andrew C Campbell	15 April 1917	-	1 October 1917	KIA
Ray C Bridgman	1 May 1917	-	18 February 1918	103rd AS
Charles H Dolan Jnr	12 May 1917	-	18 February 1918	103rd AS
John A Drexel	12 May 1917	-	15 June 1917	Liaison
James N Hall	12 May 1917	1	18 February 1918	103rd AS
Henry S Jones	12 May 1917	1	18 February 1918	103rd AS
Arnoux de Maison-Rouge	28 May 1917	-	6 October 1917	Ill health
Douglas MacMonagle	16 June 1917	-	24 September 1917	KIA
David M Peterson	16 June 1917	1	18 February 1918	103rd AS
James R Doolittle	2 July 1917	-	17 July 1917	WIA
Louis Verdier-Fauvety	6 October 1917	-	18 February 1918	SPA124
Christopher W Ford	8 November 1917	-	18 February 1918	103rd AS

APPENDIX 2

ACES OF THE *ESCADRILLE LAFAYETTE*

Final rank and Name	N124 Victories	Other units (and victories)	Total
Maj G Raoul Lufbery	16		16
Lt Edwin C Parsons	1	SPA3 (7)	8
Maj David Peterson	1	94th AS (3), 95th AS (2)	6
Lt Col William Thaw	2	103rd AS (3)	5

APPENDIX 3

N124/SPA124 *LAFAYETTE* SERIALS

Nieuports

Serial Number	Type	Pilot(s)	Remarks
574	11	Sgt Norman Prince	'P' marking
1116	11	Sgt Norman Prince	'P' marking
1154	16	Sgt Elliot Cowdin	'C' marking
1205	11	Adj W Bert Hall	'H' and *BERT* marking
1208	11	Sgt Paul Pavelka	'PV' monogram
1247	11	Sgt Clyde Balsley	'Lone Star' motif; WIA 19 June 1916
1248	11	Adj W Bert Hall	'H' and *BERT* marking
1256	11	Sgt G Raoul Lufbery	'RL' monogram
1286	11	Sgt Dudley Hill	Rectangle marking
1286	11	Sgt Lawrence Rumsey	*RUM* marking
1290	11	Sgt Lawrence Rumsey	*RUM* marking
1292	11	Sgt James R McConnell	*MAC*, later 'Hot Foot' marking
1313	11	Sgt James R McConnell	'Hot Foot' marking
1334	11	Sgt Victor Chapman	KIA 23 June 1916
1434	16	Sgt C Chouteau Johnson	Dice marking
1454	11	Sous-Lt Kiffin Rockwell	'R' marking
1490	17	Sous-Lt Charles Nungesser	July 1916
1572	17	Capt Georges Thenault	Butterfly marking
1582	17	Lt William Thaw	'T' marking
1645	21	Sgt G Raoul Lufbery	*L...Y* marking
1803	17	Lt William Thaw	'T' marking
1811	17	Sgt Kiffin Rockwell	'R' marking; KIA 23 September 1916
1844	17	Sgt G Raoul Lufbery	3 coup marks
1962	17	Sgt Edmond C C Genet	KIA 16 April 1917
1977	17	Adj Robert Soubiran	'S' marking
1993	17	Sgt Walter Lovell	Inverted chevron marking
2055	17	Sgt J R McConnell	KIA 19 March 1917
2551	17	Sgt Edwin C Parsons	March 1917
3578	23	Sgt A C Campbell	-
3616	24bis	Cpl James R Doolittle	Injured 17 July 1917
3772	24bis	Sgt A C Campbell	*BAT* marking
4598	24	Sgt T M Hewitt Jnr	'H' marking

SPAD VII/XIIIs

Serial Number	Type	Pilot(s)	Remarks
156	VII	Thenault, Lufbery	Butterfly, 3 coup marks
161	VII	Masson, de Laage	6 November 1916
221	VII	Parsons, Johnson, Campbell	-
238	VII	Lufbery, Willis, Dugan	5 January 1917

242	VII	Thaw, Willis, Marr	2 January 1917
331	VII	Cpl Stephen Bigelow	1 May 1917; 'Eyes' camshaft covers
387	VII	Adj Robert Soubiran	Diamond marking
		Sgt S Bigelow	WIA 18 August 1917
525	XIII	Thaw, Lovell	1 October 1917
1266	VII	Sgt Stephen Bigelow	22 March 1917
1331	VII	Sgt Kenneth Marr	'M' marking
1385	VII	Lt Alfred de Laage de Meux	18 May 1917
1386	VII	Cpl James N Hall	WIA, FTL 26 June 1917
1420	VII	Adj Robert Soubiran	-
1456	VII	Lt William Thaw	'T' marking
1515	VII	Lt Alfred de Laage de Meux	KIC 23 May 1917
1615	VII	Sgt Harold B Willis	Green 'W,' PoW 18 August 1917
1621	VII	A A de Maison-Rouge, R L Rockwell, J N Hall	2 coup marks.
1777	VII	Masson, Lufbery, Marr, Jones, Thaw	red Swastika
1859	VII	Sgt Dudley Hill	3 October 1917
1930	XIII	Sgt Kenneth Marr	3 October 1917
1932	XIII	Adj Robert Soubiran	15 October 1917
2119	VII	Cpl Douglas MacMonagle	KIA 24 September 1917
2128	VII	Lufbery, Soubiran	21 August 1917
3024	VII	Verdier-Fauvety, Lachat (French SPA124)	-
3141	VII	Capt Dudley Hill	
3148	VII	1Lt Charles H Dolan	*CHD*, to 103rd AS, Feb-May 1918
3198	VII	Capt Robert Soubiran	'RS', to 103rd AS, Feb-May 1918
4239	VII	Sgts Parsons, Masson	17 September 1917 (Tricolour band?)
4245	VII	Sgt Andrew C Campbell	KIA 1 October 1917
4274	VII	Sgt Kenneth Marr	20 October 1917

COLOUR PLATES

1

Nieuport 11 N1454 of Cpl Kiffin Rockwell, N124, Luxeuil-les-Bains, May 1916

One of the original members of N124, Kiffin Rockwell scored the unit's first victory when he downed an LVG on 18 May 1916.

2

Nieuport 16 N1154 of Sgt Elliot C Cowdin, N124, Luxeuil-les-Bains, May 1916

Already the victor over one enemy aeroplane during his previous service in N65, Elliot Cowdin seemed a natural choice to be assigned a Nieuport 16 with the 110-hp Le Rhône engine. Cowdin became a disciplinary problem, however, and was eventually removed from the *escadrille* roster, officially due to 'ill health', on 25 June 1916.

3

Nieuport 11 N1116 of Sgt Norman Prince, N124, Luxeuil-les-Bains, May 1916

'Nimmie' Prince used his initials on this and another Nieuport 11, N574. He was flying a Nieuport 17 when he scored his third victory on 10 October 1917 and his fourth during the Oberndorf raid two days later, but suffered a fatal landing accident during his return.

4

Nieuport 11 (serial unknown) of Sgt Pierre Didier Masson, N124, Luxeuil-les-Bains, May 1916

The cruciform motif that adorns the fuselage of this machine has been identified as being applied by Masson. A former mercenary pilot for Mexican Maj Gen Alvaro Obregón, Masson made one of the first bombing attacks against a ship in 1913. Later, flying a Nieuport 17, he scored his only victory under extraordinary circumstances during the Oberndorf raid on 12 October 1916.

5

Nieuport 11 N1205 of Sgt Weston Bert Hall, N124, Behonne, May 1916

Hall marked his first fighter with his last initial on the fuselage upper decking and his first name in mirror image on one side – a theme that would recur on subsequent aircraft. Personality differences with his squadronmates led to his leaving the *Escadrille Américaine*, but not before he had scored the unit's second victory on 22 May 1916, and another on 23 July.

6

Nieuport 11 N1292 of Sgt James R McConnell, N124, Behonne, May 1916

Initially marking this aeroplane with his nickname 'Mac', Jimmy McConnell later decorated it with a footprint, which referred to the 'Hot Foot Society' that he had belonged to while attending the University of Virginia.

7

Nieuport 11 N1247 of Sgt H Clyde Balsley, N124, Behonne, June 1916

Soon after painting his Texan 'Lone Star' emblem on his aeroplane, Balsley became N124's first casualty when he was grievously wounded on 16 June 1916 whilst attacking a formation of Aviatiks. He force-landed this aircraft between the French and German lines, the scout ending up on its back and eventually being destroyed by artillery fire.

8

Nieuport 17 N1490 of Sous-Lt Charles Nungesser, N124, Behonne, July 1916

Placed on enforced leave from his regular *escadrille* (N65) due to recent injuries, Nungesser attached himself to N124 for two weeks, during which he added an Aviatik to the unit's tally on 21 July 1916 – his 11th victory. Nungesser's aeroplane at this time was a typical early Nieuport 17, with green and brown camouflage and a non-rotating *cône de pénétration* attached via the propeller shaft. The latter was removed on subsequent Nieuport scouts in an effort to improve engine cooling.

9

Nieuport 11 N1256 of Sgt G Raoul Lufbery, N124, Behonne, July 1916

Lufbery scored at least some of his first four victories in Nieuport 11 N1256, which bore a white monogram of his initials. Thought to be his first scout, it bore the two-tone sprayed-on uppersurface camouflage seen on many early Nieuport 11s. This took the form of dark brown and a greyish-green in meandering large patterns on the uppersurfaces, while undersides were clear doped, or sometimes light blue. The cowling remained bright, unpainted aluminium, the wheelcovers were clear doped and the interplane V-struts varnished wood.

10

Nieuport 11 N1286 of Sgt Dudley L Hill, N124, Behonne, summer 1916

Photographed on its nose after a landing mishap, Hill's Nieuport was decorated with simple white squares.

11

Nieuport 11 N1208 of Sgt Paul Pavelka, N124, Behonne, summer 1916

Pavelka's aeroplane featured an unusual camouflage pattern that was more distinctive than his red 'PV' monogram. Later transferring to the Salonika front, Pavelka died on 12 November 1917 of injuries that he had sustained in a horse-riding accident the previous day.

12

Nieuport 16 N1434 of Sgt Charles Chouteau Johnson, N124, Behonne, summer 1916

Following Cowdin's departure from N124, his Nieuport was flown by Johnson, who applied 'snake eyes' dice to the fuselage sides and the wheel hubs. 'Chute' Johnson scored his sole confirmed victory on 26 April 1917.

13

Nieuport 21 N1645 of Sgt G Raoul Lufbery, N124, Behonne, summer 1916

The Nieuport 21 combined the fuselage of a 17 with the wings, cowling and 80-hp Le Rhône engine of an 11. Most were used as fighter trainers, but a few reached the front, although it is doubtful that Lufbery scored any of his victories with this machine.

14

Nieuport 17 N1844 of Adjutant G Raoul Lufbery, N124, Cachy, late October 1916

Nieuport 17s were flown by all four N124 pilots participating in the Oberndorf raid on 12 October 1916, although the so-called 'Seminole' Indian head (Seminoles did not wear the feathered head-dress depicted on the insignia) was not adopted until later in the month. The red 'coup marks', used as a personal marking, were originally applied to a Plains Indian warrior's horse to represent enemies who he struck with a short quirt, without killing them.

15

SPAD VII S156 of Capitaine Georges Thenault, N124, Cachy, November 1916

One of the first SPAD VIIs to arrive at N124, this machine bore Thenault's butterfly emblem near the cowling and the three coup marks associated with Lufbery, indicating that both the commander and the unit's top ace shared the new fighter until more SPADs were delivered to N124.

16

Nieuport 17 N1977 of Sgt Robert Soubiran, N124, Ravenal, March 1917

Bob Soubiran had an ongoing penchant for personalising his aircraft, starting with N1977, which had his initial in black, a thin blue fuselage stripe and a thick red one. Soubiran also took a wealth of photos of the *escadrille*.

17

Nieuport 17 N1993 of Sgt Walter Lovell, N124, Ravenal, March 1917

Lovell was photographed standing beside this aircraft, and he later flew a SPAD VII adorned with a red diagonal band, suggesting a certain commonality of motifs.

18

Nieuport 17 (serial unknown) of Sgt Edwin C Parsons, N124, Ravenal, March 1917

Edwin Parsons' aeroplane was allegedly written off while being flown by Kenneth Marr, who overshot the landing field and ended up flipped over on his back on a nearby railway embankment. Parsons' initials were red and the fuselage bands either red or red, white and blue.

19

Nieuport 17 (serial unknown) of Sgt Willis B Haviland, N124, Ham, spring 1917

Willis Haviland shared in a victory with Thaw and Johnson on 26 April 1917. He later went on to command the US Naval Air Station at Porto Corsini, in Italy, where he distinguished himself with his aggressive use of the unit's Macchi flying boats over the Adriatic in 1918.

20

Morane Saulnier P MS1112 of Sgt Ronald W Hoskier and Cpl Jean Dressy, N124, Ham, April 1917

Ron Hoskier was convinced that two-seaters made the best fighters, and he used this Morane Saulnier P for that purpose on 23 April 1917. Although he and Lt Alfred de Laage de Meux's orderly, Cpl Jean Dressy, reportedly put up a splendid fight, they were finally shot down and killed probably by Ltn Wilhelm Schunke of *Jasta* 20.

21

SPAD VII S331 of Cpl Stephen S Bigelow, N124, Ham, May 1917

Displaying one of the earliest 'Sioux Indian' head insignias, as well as eyes on the engine's camshaft covers, SPAD S331 was known to have been flown by Cpl Bigelow on 1 May 1917, although it is not certain whether it was his regular aeroplane. In practice, *escadrille* pilots flew whichever scout was available, especially when supporting Allied ground offensives (or opposing German ones), when they could fly as many as three missions during the course of a day.

22

Nieuport 23 N3578 of Sgt Andrew Courtney Campbell, SPA124, Chaudun, July 1917

The embodiment of the 'devil-may care' *Lafayette* pilot, Campbell swiftly made a name for himself when the lower left wing of this Nieuport 23 tore off in flight on 7 July 1917, and he managed to nurse the aeroplane down to a safe landing. He subsequently looked more amused than unsettled by the incident.

23

Nieuport 24bis N3772 of Sgt Andrew Courtney Campbell, SPA124, Chaudun, July 1917

Campbell was also photographed with this Nieuport 24bis, although the significance of its personal markings remains unknown. After surviving a mid-air collision with Lt Antoine Arnoux de Maison-Rouge's aeroplane – leading to the departure of SPA124's highly-strung executive officer – Campbell was flying a SPAD when his considerable luck ran out in combat on 1 October 1917.

24

Nieuport 24 N4598 of Cpl Thomas M Hewitt Jnr, SPA124, Chaudun, July 1917

In contrast to such fearless squadronmates as Victor Chapman and 'Court' Campbell, 'Jerry' Hewitt never lived up to everyone's expectations, including his own. Joining SPA124 amid heavy combat activity, he was unnerved early on and became so unreliable that Thenault had him transferred out of the unit on 17 September 1917.

25

SPAD VII S1456 of Lt William Thaw, N124, Chaudun, June 1917

Thaw's Nieuport 11s may have sported a white disk as a personal marking, but Nieuport 17 N1582 and every one of his aeroplanes thereafter (including S1456) were marked with his initial, usually in red.

26

SPAD VII S1615 of Sgt Harold Buckley Willis, SPA124, Senard, 18 August 1917

Brought down and credited to Ltn Wilhelm Schulz of *Jasta* 16 while flying this machine, Willis escaped captivity more than a year later. Former Pfalz test pilot Uffz Max Holtzem tried to take off in Willis' patched up aeroplane, but only ended up crashing near the aerodrome.

27

SPAD VII (serial unknown) of Adjutant Walter Lovell, SPA124, Chaudun, autumn 1917

While not a high scorer, Lovell gained respect as a reliable flight leader, supporting both his squadron and his group mates. On 18 August 1917 he scored his only confirmed victory when he and Maréchal-des-Logis Marcel Paris of SPA65 downed an Albatros over Cierges.

28

SPAD VII S4239 of Sgt Edwin C Parsons, SPA124, Senard, autumn 1917

Known to have been on the *escadrille* roster on 17 September 1917, S4239 was flown mainly by Edwin Parsons and, to a lesser extent, by Didier Masson. Parsons downed a Rumpler for his first victory on 4 September 1917, possibly while flying this very aircraft. Unlike most of his squadronmates, he preferred to remain in French service rather than join the USAS, and he went on to score seven more victories serving with another famous French *escadrille*, SPA3.

29

SPAD VII S1621 of SPA124, Senard, autumn 1917

Bearing two red coup marks and a blue radiator cowling, S1621 typified many SPA124 aircraft that were flown by different pilots at various times – in this case, Lt Antoine Arnoux de Maison-Rouge and Sgts Robert L Rockwell and James Norman Hall.

30

SPAD VII S1777 of Sous-Lt G Raoul Lufbery, SPA124, Chaudun, October 1917

First flown by Dider Masson on 28 June 1917, S1777 was used mainly by him (on no fewer than 20 missions all told) until 5 October when Lufbery – who had flown two combat missions in it on 17 August – became the SPAD's principal pilot. Completing 26 missions with the scout, 'Luf' scored three confirmed victories in S1777 on 16 and 24 October and on 2 December. Kenneth Marr, Hank Jones and Bill Thaw were among a number of other SPA124 pilots who also flew this veteran machine on more than one occasion at various times.

31

SPAD VII S3198 of Capt Robert Soubiran, 103rd Aero Squadron, Ferme de la Noblette, February 1918

Originally issued in French national markings, and bearing a the red letters 'RS' within a similarly-coloured diamond, S3198 later acquired USAS markings and a white 'S' within a solid red diamond.

32

SPAD VII (serial unknown) of 1Lt Christopher W Ford, 103rd Aero Squadron, Ferme de la Noblette, March 1918

Chris Ford marked his SPAD VII with a tricolour lightning bolt, both during his time with SPA124 and in his first few months of service in the 103rd Aero Squadron. He was credited with two victories before being brought down by ground fire and taken prisoner on 15 October 1918.

33

SPAD VII S3148 of 1Lt Charles H Dolan, 103rd Aero Squadron, Bonne Maison, April 1918

'Carl' Dolan applied a *CHD* monogram to his SPADs in increasingly ornate style, carrying on that practice when SPA124 became the 103rd Aero Squadron until USAS regulations required personal motifs to be replaced by yellow numerals. S3148 was also used by 1Lt George Evans Turnure, a former *Lafayette* Flying Corps pilot who had previously flown in SPA103. Dolan scored his only confirmed victory with the 103rd on 12 October 1918.

34

SPAD VII S3141 of Capt Dudley L Hill, 103rd Aero Squadron, Bonne Maison, April 1918

As with his earlier Nieuport, Hill applied a white panel to the fuselage upper decking of his SPAD VII, although on this occasion he inscribed it with the opening bars of the US national anthem, 'The Star Spangled Banner'.

35

SPAD VII S5301 of 1Lt George Turnure, 103rd Aero Squadron, Bray Dunes, May 1918

Initially assigned to Maj William Thaw on 27 February 1918, S5301 probably figured in the three victories he scored while commanding the 103rd Aero Squadron. Later flown by 1Lt George Turnure, the scout was duly passed on to 1Lts Hobart A H Baker and Drummond Cannon before finally being turned in on 16 June 1918.

36

SPAD XIII S7714 of Capt Robert Soubiran, 103rd Aero Squadron, Lisle-en-Barrois, November 1918

As commander of the 103rd, Soubiran indulged the privilege of being able to indulge – as he had while in N124 – in flamboyantly individualistic markings, including red diamonds on the tailplane and a red 'S' on the upper wing, instead of the more regulation yellow numeral.

37

SPAD VII S5721 of Lt Alberto Lello Portela, SPA124, La Cheppe, May 1918

One of three Portuguese officers assigned to SPA124, Lello Portela was the most visible as to his nationality – and gave the longest and most distinguished service, being made a *Chevalier de la Légion d'Honneur* by the French, as well as receiving the *Croix de Guerre* with palm.

38

SPAD VII S5729 of Adjutant Václas Pilát, SPA124, La Cheppe, May 1918

A Czech volunteer in the French air service, Pilát would have been shot as a traitor had he fallen into enemy hands, since his native Bohemia was then a part of Germany's ally, the Austro-Hungarian Empire.

39

SPAD XIII S4472 of Capitaine Pavel Argeyev, SPA124, Francheville, June 1918

While flying with SPA124, Argeyev decorated all of his SPADs with the number '19', including S4472, which soon had a bust of Joan of Arc added to the diagonal white band that served as the *escadrille* insignia. After scoring his first six victories in Russia, Argeyev added nine more with SPA124 to become its second-raking ace after another, earlier foreign volunteer in the *escadrille's* ranks, G Raoul Lufbery.

BIBLIOGRAPHY

Frank W Bailey, *The 103rd Aero, USAS (Formerly Lafayette Escadrille)*, Cross & Cockade (USA) Journal, Vol 19, No 4, Winter 1978

Frank W Bailey, *L'Escadrille Jeanne d'Arc, SPA124*, Cross & Cockade (USA) Journal, Vol 19, No 4, Winter 1978

Philip C Brown, *Pavelka of the Lafayette,* Cross & Cockade (USA) Journal, Vol 19, No 2, Winter 1978

Dennis Connell and Frank W Bailey, *Victory Logs, Lafayette Escadrille and Lafayette Flying Corps*, Cross & Cockade (USA) Journal, Vol 21, No 4, Winter 1980

Howard G. Fisher, *SPAD S1777: Whose Aircraft?* Over the Front, Vol 15, No 3, Fall 2000

Norman Franks, *Sharks Among the Minnows*, Grub Street, London, 2001

Norman L R Franks, Frank W Bailey and Russell Guest, *Above the Lines*, Grub Street, London, 1993

Randal S Gaulke, translator, *Baden's Airmen Remember*, Over the Front, Vol 4, No 4, Winter 1989, pp 346-349

Dennis Gordon, *The Lafayette Flying Corps*, Schiffer Publishing Ltd, Atglen, Pa, 2000

La Vie Aérienne Illustrée, 1917-18

H D Hastings, *The Oberndorf Raid*, Cross & Cockade (USA) Journal, Vol 5, No 4, pp 365-384

Tom Walden, *James Norman Hall—The Great Adventurer (Parts II and III)*, Over the Front, Vol 17, No1, Spring 2002, and Vol 17, No 2, Summer 2002

Dale Walker, *The Ted Parsons Story*, Aviation Quarterly, Vol 4, No 1, 1978

INDEX

References to illustrations are shown in **bold**. Colour Plates are shown with page and caption locators in brackets.

Argeyev, Capitaine Pavel Vladimirovich **39** (42, 126), **104**, 104, 105, **106**, 106, 107

Bach, Cpl Jules James 7, 10-12
Baer, 1Lt Paul Frank 97-98
Balsley, Cpl (later Sgt) Horace Clyde 14-15, 16, **20**, 21, 22-24,**23**, **7** (34, 124), **120**
Barancy, Lt Henri **105**, 105, **106**
Barlet, Cpl Lucien 54
Baylies, Sgt Frank 117
Bell-Davies, Richard, VC 52, 55; 56
Bentejac, Adjutant Paul 104, **107**
Bergé, Capitaine Henri **107**, 107
Bigelow, Cpl Stephen Sohier **21** (38, 125), **66**, 66-67, **74**, **76**, **78**, 82, 84, **120**
Brandywine Creek 6
Breguet-Michelin BM IV **51**, **54**
Breguet-Michelin BM V **53**
Bridgman, Capt Ray Claflin 72, **78**, 99, **115**, 115-116, **116**, **120**
Butterworth, Flt Sub-Lt Charles H S 53

Callan, Lt Cdr John L 116, 117
Campbell Jnr, Sgt Andrew Courtney 'Coty/Court' **22**, **23** (38,125), 70-71, **78**, 79, **80**, 85, 89-90, **90**, **120**
Campbell, 1Lt Douglas 113, **114**
Caudron G 3: **77**
Cazenove de Pradines, Adjutant Pierre de **86**
Champagny, Capitaine Henri Nompère de **106**
Chang Hui-chang, Gen 62
Chapman, 2Lt Charles W 109
Chapman, Cpl (later Sgt) Victor **9**, **16**, 16, 17, **18**, 18, 19, 20, 21-22, 24-25, **120**
background 7, 8, 12-13
Charton, Cpl Louis 105
Collishaw, Flt Sub-Lt Raymond 53, 57
Corso, Adjutant Emmanuele **107**
Cowdin, Cpl (later Sgt) Elliot Christopher **9**, 16, **18**, 18, **20**, **22**, **23**, 25-26, **26**, **2** (33, 124), **120**
background 12, **13**, 13
Curtis, Frazier V

Dauguet, Sgt 84-85
Davis, 2Lt Philip W **108**
Desthuilleirs, Sgt **4**, 84-85
Dolan Jnr, Sgt (later 1Lt) Charles Heave 'Carl' **33** (41, 126), 74, **87**, 87-89, **88**, 100, 101, 101, **119**, **120**
Doolittle, Cpl James Ralph **78**, 79, 80-81, **120**
Douillet, Sous-Lt Louis **107**
Dressy, Cpl Jean 16, **20** (38, 43, 125), 71, **72**, 72
Drexel, Flt Sub-Lt (later Maj) John Armstrong 74, 77, **120**
Dubonnet, Maréchal-des-Logis André 117, 118
Dugan Jnr, Soldat (later 1Lt) William Edward **8**, **70**, 70, **78**, 99, **120**

Féquant, Maj Philippe 59, 69, 78, 91
Fokker D II **52**
Fokker D III **53**
Fonck, Sous-Lt René 117
Ford, 1Lt (later Col) Christopher William **32** (41, 45, 126), 94, 97, 98, 99, **100**, 100-101, **120**
France, Service Aeronautique 10
escadrilles
BM120: **51**, 52, 53, 54, 54, 56, 57
F29: 51, 52-53, 57
F123: 51, 53, 57
N65: **13**
N124 (Americaine) 16-32, **19-32**, **1-21** (33-38, 43, 124-125), **25** (39, 125), **47-63**, 47-64
N124 (Lafayette) 64-76, **65**, **67**, **69**, **71**, **73**, **74**, **75**, **79**, **80**
SPA3: 117-118
SPA124 (French unit) 96, 102, **103**, **104**, **105**
SPA124 (Lafayette) **4**, **22-24** (38-39, 125), **26-30** (39-40, 44, 125-126), **37-39** (42, 46, 126), **68**, 76, **80-96**, 80-96
VC113: **58**
Groupe de Bombardement (GB) 4: 48, 51
Groupe de Combat (GC) 13: 59-60, 70, 76, 80, 89
Groupe de Combat 21: 96, 97, 98, 104, 105-106

Gaillard de la Valdène, Brigadier Jean Pierre de 53, 57
Gement (mechanic) **82**
Genet, Cpl Edmond Charles Clinton 7-8, 65, 67, 68-69, **71**, 71, **120**
German Air Service
Bayerische Fliegerabteilung (Bavarian Flying Det.) 9 (F. F. Abt. 9b) 52, 54
KEK (Kampfeinsitzer Kommando) Ensisheim 52
KEK Habsheim (F. Fl. Abt. 48/Jasta 15) **52**, 52, **53**, 54
Giroux, Lt Ernest A 98
Green, 1Lt M Edwin 109
Gros, Dr Edmund Louis 12, 64, 110, 118

Haber, Ltn Kurt 55, 57-58
Hall, George 8-9
Hall, Cpl (later Capt) James Norman 10, 17, 63, 110, **120**
with 103rd Aero Sqn **97**, 97, **109**, 109-110, **110**
with SPA124: **77**, 78-79, 86, 88-89, **95**, 95
Hall, Sgt (later Adjutant) Weston Birch 'Bert' **9**, 16, **18**, 18, 19, **27**, **28**, 28, 29, 32, **5** (34, 43, 124), 48, 61-62, **120**
background 7, **8**, 9, 11-12, 13
Hammann, Charles H 117
Hanstein, Vzfw Ludwig 52, 53, 57
Happe, Capitaine Maurice 48, 49, 50-51, **51**, 55

Haviland, Sgt (later Lt Cdr) Willis Bradley **19** (37, 125), 59, 73, 89, 116-117, **120**
Hengst, Ltn Friedrich **108**, 109, **110**
Hewitt Jnr, Cpl Thomas Moses 'Jerry' **24** (39, 125), **70**, 70, 72, 73, 76, **120**
Hill, Cpl (later Capt) Dudley Lawrence 15, **23**, **34** (41, 45, 126), **78**, 99, **115**, 115, 116, **120**
with N124: **10** (35, 124), 48, **60**, 65
Hilz, Vzfw Ludwig 52, 53, 54
Hinkle, Sgt Edward Foote 'Pop' 30, 63, **68**, 68, **70**, 70, 76, 77, 91-92, **120**
Holtzem, Uffz Max 83, **84**, 125
Hoskier, Cpl (later Sgt) Ronald Wood **20** (38, 43, 125), 64-65, 71, **72**, 72, **120**
Hudson, 1Lt Henry 115
Huffer, Maj John **112**, 112, 114
Humières, Lt André d' 96, **105**, 105, 107

insignia
Jeanne d'Arc bust **39** (42, 126), 105-106
Seminole Indian head **60**, 61, **67**, 76, 125
Sioux (Lakota) Indian head **68**, **76**, 76, 96-97, 100-101
Izac, Lt Edouard 83-84

Johnson, Sgt Charles Chouteau 'Chute' 15, 16, 21, **26**, **27**, **12** (36, 124), 48, 73, **78**, **120**
Jones, 1Lt Clinton 115
Jones, Sgt (later 1Lt) Henry Sweet 'Hank' 74, **75**, **78**, 86, 89-90, 99, **120**

Kilani, Ltn 54
Kirschbaum, Gftr Otto **112**, 112
Kissenberth, Ltn Otto **52**, 52, 53, 55-56, **57**, 58, 88, **89**

Laage de Meux, Capt Alfred de **9**, 16, **27**, 29, 51, 68, **70**, 70, 74-75, **75**
Lafayette, Capt Marie Joseph Paul Yves Roch Gilbert du Motier, marquis de 6
Lamy, Capitaine **91**
Leite, Capitaine Santos 102, 104
Lemaire, Lt **51**
Lovell, Sgt (later Maj) Walter **17** (37, 125), **27** (39, 126), **67**, 67-68, **78**, **82**, 82, 93-94, **94**, **120**
Lufbery, Sgt (later Maj) Gervais Raoul Victor 'Luf' **120**
background 7, 8, 9-10, 13-14
death 112, **113**, 113, 114
Oberndorf raid 50, 55, 58
with 94th Aero Sqn **108**, 108, 109, **111**
with N124 (Escadrille Americaine) 20-21, **23**, **27**, 29, 29-30, **9** (35, 124), **13**, **14** (36, 124-125), 47, 48-49, **56**, 63
with N124 (Escadrille Lafayette) 65, 66, 68, **70**, 70, 71, **73**, 73, 74
with SPA124: **30** (40, 126), 77, **78**, 84, 87, 88, 91-92, **92**, **93**, 93, 94-95, **95**, 107
Luneau, Soldat 54

MacMonagle, Douglas **78**, 87-88, **88**, **120**
Maison-Rouge, Lt Antoine Arnoux de 76, **78**, 85-86, 125
Marchand, Cpl 55
Marr, Cpl (later Capt) Kenneth Archibald **4**, **69**, 69, **70**, 84, 86-87, 97, **120**, 125
with 94th Aero Sqn 110, **114**, 114-115
Marsh, 1Lt Henry B 106-107, **107**
Marshall, Emil 61, 67
Masson, Sgt Pierre Didier 14, **65**, 67, **74**, **120**
Oberndorf raid 55, 58
with N124 (Escadrille Americaine) **25**, 25, **26**, **27**, **32**, **4** (34, 124), **55**, 55, 58, **63**
with SPA124: **78**, 78, 91
McConnell, Cpl (later Sgt) James Rogers 'Jimmy' 15, 68-69, **120**
with N124 (Escadrille Americaine) **9**, 16, 16, 18, **21**, 21, **23**, 26, 27, 28, 32, **6** (34, 124), 32, 32, **4** (34, 124), **55**, 55, 58, **63**
Memorial de l'Escadrille Lafayette, Parc Revue, Villeneuve l'Etang 58, 113, 118, **119**
Morane Saulnier P **20** (38, 43, 125), 71-72, **72**
Mottay, Maréchal-des-Logis Léon 55

Naval Air Station Porto Corsini 116, 117, 125
Nieuport 10: **16**
Nieuport 11: **8**, **13**, 17, **19**, **4** (34, 124), **59**
N1116: **20**, **22**, **3** (33, 124)
N1205: 18, **28**, **5** (34, 43, 124)
N1208: **30**, **11** (35, 124)
N1247: **20**, 21, **7** (34, 124)
N1256: **20**, **9** (35, 124)
N1286: **20**, 21, **10** (35, 124)
N1290: **21**, 21, 32
N1292: **21**, **6** (34, 124)
N1454: **1** (33, 124)
Nieuport 16: 17, 18, **20**, 21, **22**, **23**, **26**, **2** (33, 124), **12** (36, 124)
Nieuport 17: **18**, **19** (37, 125), 47, **60**, **65**, **69**
N1490: **27**, **31**, **8** (35, 124)
N1582: **40**
N1803: **56**
N1811: **49**, 49
N1844: **14** (36, 125), **63**
N1977: **16** (37, 125), **71**
N1993: **17** (37, 125), **67**
Nieuport 21: **13** (36, 124)
Nieuport 23: **22** (38, 125), **79**, 79, **80**
Nieuport 24: **24** (39, 125), **80**
Nieuport 24bis **23** (38, 125), 80, **81**, **90**
Nieuport 28: **108**, **109**, **110**, **111**, **114**, 114
Nieuport 28.C1: 108-109

Nordhoff, Charles Bernard 110
Nungesser, Sous-Lt Charles **26**, **27**, 27-28, **31**, 31, **8** (35, 124), 58, 103-104

Oberndorf-am-Neckar raid 50-58

Parsons, Sgt (later Sous-Lt) Edwin Charles 'Ted' 9, 14, 113-114, **117**, 118, 119, **120**
with N124 (Escadrille Lafayette) **18** (37, 125), 65, 68-69, **69**, **70**
with SPA124: **28** (40, 44, 126), 76, **78**, 81-82, 84, 88, 95
Pavelka, Sgt Paul 'Skipper' **7**, 10, 30, 30-31, **11** (35, 124), **47**, 60-61, 63-64, **64**, **120**
Paversick, Lt F X 111
Perroneau, Adjutant Henri **86**
Peterson, Sgt (later Maj) David McKelvie **4**, **78**, 84-85, **85**, 97, 109, **111**, 111, **120**
Pfleiderer, Ltn 54, 55
Pilât, Adjutant Václav (Wenceslas) **38** (42, 126), **102**, 103, 104-105, **105**, 106, **107**, 107
Portela, Cpl Alberto Lello **37** (42, 46, 126), 102, **103**, 104-105, 106
Pourpe, Marc 10, 13, 95
Prince, Sgt (later 1Lt) Frederick Henry **59**, 59, 60, **65**, 67, **120**
Prince, Sgt (later Sous-Lt) Norman 'Nimmie' **9**, **12**, **16**, 16, 17, **18**, 18, 20, **23**, **26**, 26, **27**, **3** (33, 124), 48, **120**
background 8, 12, 13
Oberndorf raid 50, 54, 56, 58
Putnam, 1Lt David E **115**

Raymond, Capitaine Georges 117
Regnier, Col Henri 16
Rickenbacker, 1Lt Edward V 109, 110, **114**, 114
Ritscherle, Vztr (later Ltn) Karl 90
Robert, Lt Marcel **105**, 105, **106**, 106
Rockwell, Cpl (later Sous-Lt) Kiffin Yates **9**, **16**, 16, 17, **18**, 18, 19, 19-20, 22, 25, **27**, **28**, 32, **1** (33, 124), 48, 49, 49, 61, **120**
background **6**, 6, 7, 8, 10, 13
Rockwell, Paul Ayres 6, **7**, 7, 11, 18, 32, 62, 119
Rockwell, Capt Robert Locherbie 'Doc' 47-48, **78**, 88, 99, 101, **114**, **120**
Rousset, Sous-Lt Gaston 104
Royal Naval Air Service (RNAS), 3 Wing 48, 51, 52, 53, 55, **57**, 57
Rumsey Jnr, Sgt Lawrence Dana 15-16, **20**, **21**, 21, **27**, 60, 62-63, **120**

Sayaret, Adjutant Victor 29
Scheibe, Ltn Kurt **112**, 112
Schulz, Ltn Wilhelm 83, 125
Sejourné, Lt Louis **91**
Simer, Adjutant Salah **107**
Simson, Ltn 54, 55
Sopwith 11/2 Strutter **102**
Soubiran, Sgt (later Maj) Robert 6-7, **16** (37, 125), 59, **63**, **71**, **78**, **99**, 99, **120**
with 103rd Aero Sqn **31** (40, 126), **36** (42, 46, 126), **101**, 101
SPAD VII **23** (41, 45, 126), **100**, **104**, 105
S156: **15** (36, 125), **71**
S331: **21** (38, 125), **74**, **76**
S1331: **4**
S1456: **25** (39, 125), **74**
S1615: **26** (39, 44, 125), **83**, 83, **84**
S1621: **29** (40, 126)
S1777: **30** (40, 126), **74**, **75**, **95**
S3141: **34** (41, 45, 126)
S3198: **31** (40, 126), **33**(41, 126), **99**
S4239: **28** (40, 44, 126)
S5301: **35** (41, 126), **98**
S5721: **37** (42, 46, 126), **103**, 104
S5729: **38** (42, 126)
SPA124: **27** (39, 126), **68**, **73**, **81**, **85**, **87**, **88**, **94**, **96**
SPAD XIII **36** (42, 46, 126), **39** (42, 126), **97**, 99, **101**, **105**, **114**, **120**

Talmage, Gertrude 8, 69
Thaw II, Sous-Lt (later Lt Col) William 'Bill' 66, 68, **70**, 73, **74**, **78**, **86**, 99-100, 118, **120**
background 6, 7, 8, 10, 11, 13
with 103rd AS **35** (41, 126), 96, 97, **98**, 98
with N124 (Escadrille Americaine) **8**, **9**, 16, **18**, 19, 20, **27**, **25** (39, 125), **47**, 48, 48, 50, 61
Thenault, Capitaine (later Col) Georges **9**, 11, **16**, 16, 17, 19, 22, 25-26, 30, **15** (36, 125), 118
dog (Fram) **9**, **70**, **78**
with SPA124: **65**, **70**, 71, **75**, **78**, 87, 96
Turnure, 1Lt George Evans 97, 126
Tyndall, 1Lt Frank B 115

Udet, Vzfw Ernst **53**, 53, **54**, 54, 58
United States Army Air Service (USAS) 108
Aero Squadrons
22nd 115, **116**
93rd **114**
94th 108, **108**, **109**, 109, **110**, **111**
95th 108
103rd **31-36**(40-42, 45-46, 126), **96**, 96-97, **97**, 98, 99, **100**, 100, **101**
Pursuit Group, 3rd 99-100

Verdier-Fauvety, Lt Louis 90-91, **91**, 103-104
Viallet, Maréchal-des-Logis **4**, 84-85
Villeneuve, Capitaine Lucien Couret de 96
Vimal du Monteil, Sous-Lt Henri 104
Voisin 8 (Canon) **58**

Weeks, Alice Standish 20, 32, **61**
Willis, Sgt Harold Buckley **26**(39, 44, 125), **67**, 68, 76, **78**, 82-84, **83**, **120**
Winslow, 2Lt Alan F 109
Wintgens, Ltn Kurt **24**, 25